Paul Gordon was born in Glasgow and studied law at Glasgow University. Formerly research officer for the Scottish Council for Civil Liberties, he now lives in London and researches for the Runnymede Trust. Paul Gordon has written extensively on policing, race and civil liberties. His books include, *White Law: Racism in the Police, Courts and Prisons* (Pluto Press, 1983), *Racism and Discrimination: a select bibliography 1970–1983*, with Francesca Klug (Runnymede Trust, 1983), and *Causes for Concern: British Criminal Justice on Trial*, co-edited with Phil Scraton (Penguin, 1984).

Paul Gordon

# Policing Immigration

Britain's Internal Controls

Pluto Press

London and Sydney

First published in 1985 by Pluto Press Limited,
The Works, 105a Torriano Avenue, London NW5 2RX
and Pluto Press Australia Limited, PO Box 199, Leichhardt,
New South Wales 2040, Australia

Cover designed by James Beveridge

Typeset by Wayside Graphics, Clevedon, Avon
Printed in Great Britain by Guernsey Press, Guernsey C.I.

British Library Cataloguing in Publication Data
Gordon, Paul, *1954* –
   Policing immigration: Britain's internal controls.
   1. Race discrimination — Great Britain
   2. Minorities — Great Britain   3. Great Britain — Race relations
   I. Title
   305.8′00941      DA125.A1

ISBN 0 86104 623 4

# Contents

# Acknowledgements

Since this book really began life as a pamphlet, *Passport Raids and Checks* (published by the Runnymede Trust in 1981), it is only appropriate to record my thanks once again to those who offered advice and criticism during that project, particularly the Joint Council for the Welfare of Immigrants. The Council's files yielded much of the material used in that pamphlet and have proved useful yet again in this book. Two books have also proved immensely useful for their accounts of the law – Ian Macdonald: *Immigration Law and Practice in the United Kingdom* (Butterworth, 1983) and Wendy Collins and Hugo Storey: *Immigrants and the Welfare State* (National Association of Citizens Advice Bureaux, 1983). Several long-suffering friends and colleagues have allowed themselves to be imposed upon once again: Steve Connor, Chris Pounder and Frances Webber each read parts of the manuscript and offered useful corrective advice; and, at Pluto, Paul Crane was, once again, an encouraging, sympathetic and tactful editor. I am particularly grateful to Hilary Arnott and Danny Reilly for their constant advice, criticism and friendship throughout the time this book was being written.

# Introduction

..., the *Financial Times*, a newspaper not noted for hysteri-
... commented on new British immigration proposals
... How far is it from there to the pass laws?'.[1] What
... to make this comparison with the apartheid
re... ...frica was the report, signed by both Labour
and ... ... of the Parliamentary Select Committee
on Race ... Immigration.

The Co... ... recommendations about immigration controls which wo... operate *after* entry, *within* the UK were particularly worrying. The Committee had said not only that the police
and the immigration service should be given more resources to
deal with breaches of immigration law, and that sanctions should
be enforced against businesses which employed people who were
either illegal immigrants or not entitled to work, but also that the
government should establish an inquiry to consider a fully-
fledged system of internal controls within the UK. The Committee did not spell out what such a system would involve but it
was clear that it would be similar to other European systems and
would require everyone, or at least those subject to control, to
produce an identity card if required by a police officer or other
state official.

In the end, as we shall see, there was no such inquiry. The
Labour government of the day, although clearly in agreement
with the general direction of the Select Committee's report,
rejected the idea. The Conservative Party pledged to set up such
an inquiry, but has not in fact done so. This is not because of any
change of heart on the part of the Conservative government.
There is simply no need for an inquiry, since a system of such
controls has been quietly developing away from the public gaze.

This observation is not new. In 1978, for example, the Joint Council for the Welfare of Immigrants, the immigration casework and campaigning body, while welcoming the government's rejection of the idea of an inquiry into a system of internal control, pointed out that such a system was already being developed. It was this, JCWI said, which needed investigating.

It would be appropriate at this point therefore to be clear about what is meant by 'internal controls'. There is a tendency to equate internal controls with the practice of passport checking, for example by the police or social security offices. But this is to confuse cause and symptom: passport checking is not the motive behind internal control, but a sign that it is happening. Instead we have to define internal controls as any aspect of law or administration related in any way to immigration status which operates *within* the UK. This includes perhaps the most obvious aspects of internal immigration control such as measures taken to trace and apprehend those who may be in breach of the immigration laws. But it also covers the relationship between immigration law and other areas such as employment, housing and the welfare state. The overall effect is the questioning, restricting and controlling of the rights, not just of those who *are* immigrants, but those who are commonly assumed to be, because they are black.

Such controls, as we shall see, have existed in Britain since the early nineteenth century, although it is really only in the past ten years or so that anything like a *system* of control has come to be developed. Notwithstanding the vigilance, monitoring and campaigning of the Joint Council for the Welfare of Immigrants and others, this development has gone largely unnoticed or if noticed, largely unopposed and unchallenged. One of the reasons for this is no doubt the relative lack of publicity given to the issue. It is clear from talking to advice workers and others that the few cases which are reported are only the tip of the iceberg and that many more instances simply go unreported. Nevertheless, there have been enough cases reported to indicate that black people are treated very differently from white people. They have been subjected to 'passport raids' by police and immigration officers and required to produce passports by police officers, social security officials, hospital clerks and administrators, and schools; their right to be in the country has been questioned; their entitlement to welfare benefits and services has been challenged. The law itself has institutionalised a division – creating one class of people who, although entitled to be here, are not entitled to the same rights as others.

Yet the issue of internal immigration controls is not one of specialised concern. It has implications which range much wider than one aspect of a particular law. In the first place, because internal immigration controls affect not only immigrants but all black people in the UK, they reinforce the division in society between black and white, potentially subjecting all the former to procedures and processes which do not apply to the latter. Secondly, the operation of internal controls has had, and continues to have, serious implications for the civil liberties and rights of the population generally. If one group of people can be defined as 'different' from the population at large, and then subjected to processes and treatment which are also 'different', then such methods can more easily be extended to other 'different' groups, for the first line of resistance is broken and a precedent set. In other words, internal immigration controls are an issue which should concern not just those working to change immigration laws but all who are challenging state racism and defending civil liberties against the encroachments of the state.

This book charts the development and present state of internal controls and tries to show their effects on Britain's black community in the context of the changing nature of racism in Britain. The early origins of internal controls, on black seamen in the nineteenth century and aliens in the early twentieth century, are shown in Chapter 1. Chapter 2 looks at the application of immigration controls, including internal controls, to black people in the 1960s and 1970s, particularly the early impact of the Immigration Act of 1971, which remains the basis of the present law. Chapter 3 examines the changes in state racism in the late 1970s and how these led to an even greater emphasis on internal controls, and Chapter 4 shows how this emphasis was implemented within the welfare state, in the areas of education, health, housing and social security. Finally, Chapter 5 looks at current plans and developments in internal controls, at what the future might hold, and at what needs to be done if internal controls are to be combated effectively.

# 1. Origins

Internal controls have been an important part of the modern system of immigration laws since their introduction at the beginning of the twentieth century. Almost a century before, internal controls had been imposed on a particular group of black people – Asian seamen on British ships, traditionally known (until Indian independence in 1947) as lascars. Both these forms of internal control were precedents for the current system which has been developing since 1962 and affects the lives of many people living in the UK today.

In response to a minor public outcry about the numbers of destitute lascars in London during the early nineteenth century, provision was made by the government in the East India Trade Act of 1813 compelling the East India Company to provide food, clothing and necessary accommodation for 'Asiatic sailors' until such time as they could be taken back to India. This measure avoided any cost to the state of maintaining those who were destitute. The provisions were repeated in an Act of 1823 which also made a racial division between British subjects who were seamen. Lascars and other Asian sailors were not deemed to be British, even though seamen born in the West Indies were to be regarded 'as much British seamen as a white man would be'. The reasoning behind the Act was again concern at the numbers of lascars being discharged from ships in the UK who found themselves destitute. The Act forbade the discharge of lascars in Britain and allowed them to be paid less than seamen officially regarded as British. However, the prohibition had unforeseen consequences for the shipowners and the British economy. Since lascars were not British, they could not crew a ship sailing *from* Britain. Shipowners therefore had to employ two crews – one crew of lascars to sail from the ⸻ sub-continent and another to sail back to the sub-contine⸻ ⸻ge the first crew. Ships thus had to earn double fre⸻ ⸻heir way, and more than one shipowner complaine⸻ ⸻ of Lords Committee in 1847–48 that this double cr⸻ ⸻ed as a 'total prohibition' on the importation of co⸻ ⸻y rates of freight.[1] Such complaints led directly to a⸻ ⸻ament, passed in 1849, which made lascars British ⸻ ⸻e on board ship.

Lascars we⸻ ⸻ver, to be prevented from remaining in Britain. Th⸻ ⸻hipping Act of 1894 provided for articles of agreemen⸻ ⸻ied with lascars binding them to return to their countries o⸻ ⸻in. A ship's master or owner could be fined £30 if an Asian or African seaman was brought to the UK and, within six months, was in receipt of public funds or convicted of vagrancy. In addition, the Secretary of State was bound to repatriate or otherwise provide for all destitute Indian seamen. These provisions lasted well into the twentieth century and were only repealed by the Merchant Shipping Act of 1970.

The First World War led to a considerable increase in the number of black (and Chinese) seamen on British ships. Over 8,000 merchant seamen joined the armed forces, while a further 9,000 seamen, deemed to be 'enemy aliens', lost their jobs and were replaced by black and Chinese workers. This was especially true during 1915–1917 when wages were increased and labour was recruited in the colonies. Competition for scarce work was one of the main factors behind the post-war anti-black riots in Liverpool and Cardiff which occurred in 1919. The Assistant Chief Constable of Liverpool, for example, in a letter to the Home Office, blamed the riots on 'blacks interfering with white women, capturing a portion of the labour market . . .'. Both he and the Chief Constable of Cardiff recommended repatriation, 'compulsory . . . or otherwise', as the answer. The Home Office pointed out that compulsory repatriation of people who were, after all, British subjects was not possible. It added, nevertheless, that it was 'considered desirable that so far as possible all unemployed men should be induced to return to their own countries as quickly as possible'. In 'suitable cases' this could be achieved by deportation.

In 1919 government ministers seriously considered repatriation as a solution to the problem of unemployment and the presence of black seamen. They noted that the mere provision of ships had been an insufficient inducement for people to leave and they recommended the creation of committees at main ports to collect information on the local black population and those willing to be repatriated, to publicise existing repatriation schemes, and to impress on individuals 'the advisability of accepting repatriation'. At the same time, the Ministry of Shipping made a 'special offer' to black seamen of the same 'resettlement gratuity' as had been made to white colonial citizens.[2]

This attempt to encourage repatriation failed. In 1921, for example, the Home Office made arrangements to repatriate 700 seamen from various ports. It is not clear exactly how many went, but figures show that none of the expected 25 in Swansea turned up to board ship, while in Hull only seven of an expected 38 came forward. Pressure therefore mounted for changes in the law to control the immigration of seamen to Britain. Instructions were issued to consular offices abroad not to issue certificates of British nationality to black seamen unless they produced 'unimpeachable evidence' of their status. Immigration officers were told not to allow the entry of Arab seamen who arrived as passengers unless they too could prove their claim to British nationality. The Board of Trade wanted even stricter control, saying that 'we do not want the coloured alien to be allowed leave to land even if he *is* a *bona fide* seaman in view of the unemployment among British seamen'.[3]

These administrative controls, although ostensibly applying to non-British subjects, not only reflected and fuelled popular xenophobia but also led in practice to the exclusion of British subjects who could not establish their status to the satisfaction of the immigration officer. Exactly the same situation occurred on a wider scale following the passing of the Special Restrictions (Coloured Alien Seamen) Order in 1925. The order, which was vigorously supported by the seamen's union, was the temporary culmination of the campaign to safeguard 'British jobs' at the expense of black, foreign seafarers. The order required alien seamen to register with the police. Once registered they became liable to deportation. But, as before, the restrictions also affected black seamen who were British. Many people who claimed

British status were not believed by the authorities; in Cardiff, police destroyed British passports and other evidence of nationality, thus requiring the holders to register as aliens.[4]

The controls imposed on seamen in the nineteenth and early twentieth centuries reveal a number of parallels with later developments in internal control. They were initially imposed to reduce the perceived 'social costs' of immigration and, later, to protect the 'labour market' for the indigenous white working class. Although             to be applicable only to people who were not Britis                              people were at risk. Finally, t                                    ate solution of repatriation and                              t official circles at the time, such repatri...                         lsory but could also be induced and encouraged.

Just as black seamen were accused of taking the jobs of white workers, so in the 1880s and 1890s similar charges were made against the large numbers of refugees, mainly Jews, who fled to Britain from eastern Europe and Russia. A sustained anti-immigrant, usually anti-semitic, campaign forced the government to appoint a Royal Commission on Immigration, and in 1903 it reported in favour of legislation for immigration control. The Aliens Act of 1905 which followed forbade aliens to land in Britain except at authorised ports. Immigration officers were given extensive powers to refuse entry to people regarded as 'undesirable', which generally meant those who appeared unable 'decently' to support themselves and their families and those who appeared likely to become a charge on the rates through illness or infirmity.

The Act also gave the Home Secretary considerable powers of deportation. Aliens convicted by a court could be recommended for deportation by the judge if they were unable to support themselves and their dependants. Alternatively, a court could certify that within 12 months of arrival the alien had been destitute or wanted for an extraditable crime. He or she was then liable for deportation.

These provisions were considerably extended on the outbreak of the First World War by the 1914 Aliens Restriction Act. This was rushed through parliament on the first day of the war and gave the government (formally, the King in Council) power to make orders to prohibit or restrict the entry and departure of aliens, to deport them, to require them to live in specified areas, or to order them to comply with regulations about registering with the police.

The 1914 Act was supposed　be an emergency measure, needed for the conduct of th━　　　　t at the end of hostilities in 1918 the powers conferr━　　　　were not revoked. They were extended for one yea━　　　　s Restriction (Amendment) Act of 1919 which als━　　　　1905 law; this Act, together with the 1914 legisla━　　　　wed annually until 1971. The 1919 Act was prima━　　　　d with imposing restrictions on aliens already wit━　　　　ther than with immigration. It prohibited aliens ━　　　n juries, for example, and made it a criminal offence　　　　'promote or attempt to promote industrial unrest in a　　　　n which he has not been *bona fide* engaged for at least t━　　ars'. Although it appears never to have been used, the continued existence of this provision after 1971, despite many opportunities for its repeal, presumably means that it is regarded as potentially useful. In any case, its being in force may also serve as a warning against industrial militancy.

In 1920 an Order was made under the Act extending the Home Secretary's powers to deport, on his or her own initiative, any alien whose presence s/he deemed to be not 'conducive to the public good'. A Home Office circular was sent to all chief police officers advising them that such deportations would not 'as a rule' be ordered simply where someone had been convicted but not recommended for deportation. As Andrew Nicol has pointed out, the 'rule' was very quickly broken. A Russian emigré, Bresloff, was prosecuted in 1922 for giving his passport to someone who spoke better English in order to obtain a visa. He was fined £20 for what the court regarded as a technical offence and a prosecution request for deportation was turned down. The Home Office, however, took a different view and ordered Bresloff's deportation on the ground that allowing him to remain would not be 'conducive to the public good'. The Divisional Court rejected Bresloff's application to have the order quashed.[5]

At about the same time, the Divisional Court also rejected

the argument that natural justice required that the Home Secretary give a hearing to someone s/he proposed to deport. Samuel Venicoff was ordered to be deported. He had not been convicted of any offence, although during divorce proceedings his wife had alleged that he had once lived off the immoral earnings of a prostitute. Venicoff claimed that he should be given a hearing. The court rejected his argument because the Home Secretary had made an administrative, not a judicial, decision, and he was therefore not obliged to give a hearing. As Andrew Nicol has commented, this judgement was remarkable, since in the vast majority of deportation cases the order was prompted either by offences committed on entry, or by subsequent suspected criminal conduct. Whether an alien was guilty of such offences was clearly a justiciable issue (i.e. subject to trial in a court of law) and there could be no excuse for not allowing an alien a right to be heard.[6]

Bresloff and Venicoff were to be the first of many cases which involved not only an extension of the apparent scope of the law and the rules, but also a refusal by the courts to interfere with the exercise of executive powers.

The 1920 Aliens Order also gave increased powers to immigration officers to deal with aliens who evaded immigration control. Under the 1905 Act, immigration officers could give directions for the removal of those who had been refused entry. The 1920 Order extended this to those who had never submitted themselves to investigation or questioning. This power could only be exercised within one month of an alien's entry, but this was extended to two months in 1923. Again, as Andrew Nicol has pointed out, this power of removal is 'the lineal ancestor of the present power to deport illegal entrants'.[7]

Immigration officers were not the only people to be involved in the enforcement of these early immigration controls. The Special Branch of the police also had an important part to play. The Branch had been created in the late nineteenth century to deal with the Fenian bombing campaign in Britain. When this campaign ended, however, the Special Irish Branch, as it had been known, was not disbanded. Instead it continued to monitor Irish republican activities in Britain and Ireland and widened its scope to include the activities of many political refugees who had fled to Britain. Indeed, the Special Branch had an important influence on the passage of the 1905 Aliens Act; once it came into force, the Branch became responsible to the Home Secretary for supplying intelligence reports on aliens.

The rest of the police also had a role to play in the enforcement of the immigration laws. In 1924, for example, the Home Office advised the Chief Constable of Wiltshire that a group of Chinese had recently been smuggled into the country. The Chief Constable was to organise 'a systematic search of all Chinese laundries, boarding houses etc.' and it was suggested that 'special attention should be paid to the passports and registration certificates of all Chinese'. The Chief Constable did as he was requested but asked whether he had the power to make such a search and expressed concern that some of the local Chinese were businessmen and 'well advised by members of the legal profession'. The Home Office made a conciliatory reply and noted on the file that 'the police do not as a general rule find that the absence of express powers weakens their hand'.[8]

The 1920 Aliens Order lasted, with a few amendments, until a new Order was made in 1953. This repeated many of the provisions which it replaced. For example, aliens still had to register with the police, advising them of any change of address or occupation. The Order also established the current system of work permits which required aliens seeking employment in the UK to obtain a work permit from the Ministry of Labour (now the Department of Employment). Thousands of people have come to the UK under the work permit scheme, particularly during the 1950s when Britain faced a severe shortage of labour. Even after the implementation of the first controls on Commonwealth immigrants in 1962, work permits continued to be issued in large numbers. One of the reasons for using such migrant labour was that the work permit holders had no right to settle permanently in the UK and no right to be joined by their families. It was no doubt hoped that migrant workers would return to their 'homes' when their labour was no longer required.

The basis of the work permit system was, and is, that permits were issued only for a specific job with a specific employer. Employers had to show that they were unable to recruit suitable labour from the local workforce. Normally, permits were granted for 12 months at a time, at the end of which the employer had to show that the job was still open to the employee before the Home Office would grant an extension of stay. At the end of four years in approved employment, work permit holders would normally have the conditions attached to their stay removed. The holder then acquired settled status and became 'free in the country' and able to take any job without departmental approval.

The work permit system operated as a form of control in a number of ways. Most obviously, it controlled immigration and entry into the labour market, protecting the local labour market and confining work permit holders to those jobs which even local labour could not fill, generally the least attractive and least well paid jobs. But migrant labour also served, as Sivanandan has noted, 'to absorb the shocks of alternating booms and depressions' precisely because it was migrant, seasonal and contractual, filling in the labour gaps in periods of expansion and being laid off when it was not needed. In addition, because it was foreign (the cost of education, health and welfare had been borne by the home country and not by Britain), it yielded extra profit to the employer.[9]

But the work permit system acted (and acts) also as a form of internal control. First, work permit holders had to register with the police and notify them of any change of address, employment or even marital status. Second, permit holders could not change jobs without the permission of the authorities since permits were issued for a specific job with a specific employer. Such approval could even be necessary for job changes under the same employer, where the definition in the permit was not sufficiently wide to cover the new job. Third, work permit holders could only obtain an extension of stay from the Home Office if they were still in approved employment and if their employer confirmed that they wished to continue to employ them. Work permit holders were therefore still dependent on the approval of their employers and had to avoid any conflict with them. As a consequence many were discouraged from trade union or other workplace activity. Finally, work permit holders remained liable to deportation even after they became settled, no matter how long they had lived and worked here. They could be deported, not only following conviction for a criminal offence and a court recommendation for deportation, but also if the Home Secretary considered that deportation would be conducive to the public good. Such a system of control served, as Sivanandan has observed, to prevent the integration of migrant labour into the indigenous working class and thereby to mediate class struggle.[10] But it also provided a precedent and a model for the system of internal controls which would be developed in relation to immigrants from the Commonwealth. Indeed, these early internal controls displayed many of the features which would hold true for later developments: they were imposed to reduce the social costs of immigration to the minimum; they involved the police in their enforcement; and they gave considerable powers to the executive, powers with which the courts would show a marked reluctance to interfere.

# 2. Foundations of control

Although many thousands of people, mainly Europeans, came to the UK to work in the years after the Second World War, under either the work permit system or the special European Voluntary Workers scheme, British industries still faced a severe shortage of labour. There was, however, a ready source of labour available in the countries of the Commonwealth, the colonies and former colonies. Workers for the health service, London Transport, hotels and restaurants and the foundries were actively sought in the Caribbean and the Indian sub-continent. No statistics were kept on the entry of immigrants from the Commonwealth until 1962, but some indication of the scale of immigration can be gauged from the censuses of 1951 and 1961. In that time, the population of West Indian origin rose from 15,000 to 172,000, that of Indian origin from 31,000 to 81,000 and that of Pakistani origin from 5,000 to 25,000. Throughout this period of 'laissez-faire' immigration, the extent of immigration closely matched the number of unfilled job vacancies.

By the late 1950s, however, the demand for labour was declining and, at the same time, there was increased concern at the perceived social costs of immigration, including not just the price of education and housing, but also the threat of serious social disruption such as had occurred in the anti-black riots of Nottingham and London's Notting Hill district in 1958. Discussion therefore turned to the question of immigration control. Such discussions at government level had taken place before, for example in 1948–51 under the Attlee government, but then the needs of the economy had taken precedence over the prejudices of ministers, MPs and public opinion. Ten years and more later, there was no such conflict.

In a country which no longer required the labour it had once needed, it might have been thought that the obvious response would have been to end immigration altogether. In practice, however, most western capitalist states had found that they had to have ready recourse to sources of labour should the need arise, labour which would come – and more important, go – as the needs of the economy demanded. The problem, in other words, was not one of migration but one of settlement.[1] The obvious solution, as Sivanandan has pointed out, was to change British nationality laws so as to put Commonwealth citizens on a par with aliens. This would have prevented settlement as of right, but would also have spelled 'the end of a historical relationship which ensured the continuing dependency of the colonial periphery on the centre'.[2] Britain therefore had to devise a means of controlling immigration without ending the Commonwealth relationship but, at the same time, ensure that it had a source of cheap labour when the need arose.

A partial solution lay initially in the Commonwealth Immigrants Act of 1962. The Act made all Commonwealth citizens subject to immigration control except those born in the UK and those who held UK passports which had been issued either in the UK or by a High Commission abroad. Those who were subject to control could enter the UK only if they held a Ministry of Labour employment voucher. But the Act was not concerned simply with controlling entry. It also implemented the first post-entry controls on resident Commonwealth citizens and those who would be admitted in the future. For the first time ever, Commonwealth citizens could be deported, although this power was not yet as extensive as in the case of aliens. There was no power to deport those whose departure the Home Secretary thought 'conducive to the public good', but only those who had been convicted by a court and recommended for deportation. Commonwealth citizens who had been ordinarily resident in the UK for five years acquired an immunity from deportation. Simple removal from the country was also possible where a Commonwealth citizen was refused entry but nevertheless managed to enter surreptitiously, although this could happen only if s/he was apprehended within 24 hours of landing. There was, however, no obligation on people to present themselves for examination by an immigration officer and evasion of control altogether was not an offence.

The Commonwealth Immigrants Act 1962 was the start of a process; and increasingly restrictive controls followed. The Labour government had pledged to repeal the legislation when in opposition; but in 1965 it implemented even tougher controls, cutting down on the number of Ministry of Labour vouchers issued to new immigrants and ending the issue of Category C vouchers (for unskilled work) altogether. It also promised a crackdown on illegal immigration although it provided no evidence of such illegality.

The Commonwealth Immigrants Act of 1968, which was passed primarily to withdraw the right to emigrate to Britain from East African Asians who had retained their British passports, also placed a duty on all Commonwealth immigrants to pass through immigration control. Those who did not could be prosecuted for illegal entry if the case were brought before a magistrate within six months. However, in 1973, the ruling in *Azam*'s case (see page 19) effectively extended this time limit for prosecution.

In 1969, when Commonwealth immigration controls had been in force for seven years, Labour passed an Immigration Appeals Act to appease some of the increasing criticism of the operation of the immigration controls. Despite its title, the Act considerably *strengthened* control in two ways. It was made compulsory for intending immigrants to obtain an entry clearance certificate *before* they left their country of origin. (This provision was not in the Bill when it was first published but was introduced later in the House of Commons at Committee stage by government amendment.) It also empowered the Home Secretary to deport, on his own initiative, any immigrant who broke a condition attached to entry.

This somewhat *ad hoc* approach to immigration control was fully systematised by the Immigration Act of 1971. This divided the world into patrials and non-patrials. Patrials, who were free from immigration control, were defined as citizens of the UK and Colonies who were born in the UK or had a UK-born parent or grandparent. Other citizens of the UK and colonies who had been settled in the UK and been ordinarily resident for five years when the Act came into force in January 1973 also became patrial. All others, generally speaking, became non-patrial and were subject to immigration control.

The Immigration Act of 1971 marked the virtual end of the process, begun in 1962, of transforming the status of Commonwealth citizens from immigrants and settlers to migrant workers. After January 1973, when the Act came into force, black immigration was largely limited to the dependants of those already settled in the United Kingdom.

The Act also provided for extensive internal controls on those already resident in the UK. The immunity from deportation enjoyed by Commonwealth citizens who had been living in the UK for five years now became restricted to those who were 'ordinarily resident' in the UK in 1973. (The phrase 'ordinarily resident' meant, generally speaking, having made one's home in the UK, at least so it was thought until the mid-1970s when the meaning of the phrase was challenged in the courts – (see page 76.) All other Commonwealth citizens arriving after that time were liable to deportation unless they became British citizens. They became liable to deportation if the Home Secretary deemed their presence not to be 'conducive to the public good'. If a man was deported, his wife and children could also be sent away; but in the case of a woman deportee only her children – and not her husband – were liable to such 'family deportation'.

In addition to these extensions of deportation, the 1971 Act also gave the Home Secretary authority to order the removal of anyone deemed to be an illegal entrant. The time limits which existed previously were abandoned and removal could occur no matter how long a person had been in the country. Except in a few, very limited cases, appeal against removal was possible only *after* departure.

The 1971 Act also gave the police wide powers of arrest without warrant in cases of suspected illegal entry, breach of conditions, overstaying, harbouring an illegal entrant or overstayer, and obstruction of an immigration officer or anyone else carrying out an immigration function.

The formal provisions of the Immigration Act were clearly draconian, but the original draft which was presented to parliament went even further, proposing that Commonwealth citizens, like aliens, should be required to register with the police. Many people pointed out that this would presumably require black people to carry some form of identification to distinguish those who were patrials from those who had to be registered. The proposal was dropped under pressure, but the other main provisions of the Bill remained unchanged. The law gave rise to considerable anxiety when it was being debated in parliament. Its interpretation and enforcement in practice, however, were to go beyond what most people had feared.

## Interpreting the law

Black people and others subject to the new law did not have to wait long to see what it would mean in practice for them. The Immigration Act came into effect on 1 January 1973. Within months the courts were presented with an opportunity by the immigration authorities not only to interpret the meaning of the law, but also to decide whether the law applied retrospectively, that is, to situations *before* it had come into effect.

The case of *Azam*[3] concerned three Commonwealth immigrants who had entered the UK clandestinely, avoiding immigration control. One had twice been refused entry and returned later in a small boat, landing without being detected. This was a 'continuing' offence, that is one which was held in law to last beyond the immediate date of its commission. The man was therefore an illegal entrant under the 1962 Act and could not claim to have been 'settled' in Britain by January 1973, when the 1971 Act came into effect.

The case of the other two men involved was, however, more complicated. They had entered the country clandestinely after the 1968 Act came into force, avoiding examination by an immigration officer and thereby committing an offence and becoming illegal entrants. They had not been prosecuted within the appropriate time limit and there was no way in which they could be deported or removed under the pre-1971 law. The question to be decided was explained by barrister Ian MacDonald:

> The courts had a very clear choice to make: (1) treat clandestine entrants who had committed once and for all offences as

no longer in breach of Immigration Rules, as 'settled' and therefore irremovable; or (2) treat the Act as having retrospective effect – something the courts have always said they disliked – and thus 'enable the executive in the future, to seize and imprison a Commonwealth citizen, long resident in this country and leading a blameless life, because of a summary offence he may have committed in the distant past and for which he had for years been immune from prosecution and for which he may long ago have been tried, convicted and punished'.[4]

The courts, right up the House of Lords, opted for the second choice. The Immigration Act was held to be retrospective and its powers of removal could be used against almost everyone who had entered the UK clandestinely before the law came into force. The only exceptions were people who had entered without permission before the 1968 Act and avoided apprehension for 24 hours, which was then the time limit for a prosecution.

As a result of the *Azam* decision, the Home Secretary announced in April 1974 that he would not order the removal of Commonwealth citizens who had entered the UK illegally after March 1968 and before January 1973, nor those who had entered illegally before March 1968 having been refused permission by an immigration officer. Between 1974 and 1979, 2,430 applications for this amnesty were dealt with and 621 (26 per cent) were found to be ineligible.[5] The amnesty itself effectively became a way of apprehending people alleged to be in breach of immigration law and another form of internal control.

The widening application of the Immigration Act did not stop at making its provisions retrospective. The immigration authorities and the courts also had scope to interpret what the provisions of the law actually meant in practice. This was most important in the case of the concept of 'illegal entry'. The 1971 Act defined an illegal entrant as someone who knowingly entered the UK without the leave of an immigration officer or in breach of a deportation order. There was little discussion of this when the law was being debated by parliament in 1971, but the general understanding was that an illegal entrant was someone who entered the country clandestinely, by avoiding immigration control altogether. Even the Home Secretary of the time, Reginald Maudling, referred to illegal entrants as those who 'sneak across the beaches late at night'.[6]

Within a few years of the Act coming into force, however, it became clear that the official definition went far beyond this. In two cases in 1976, the Home Office claimed that immigrants who had told lies to gain entry were illegal entrants. The claim was not tested, however, since in both cases the immigrants admitted telling lies and accepted that this made their entry illegal. As Andrew Nicol has noted, 'The novelty of the Home Office's submission did not seem to have been appreciated'.[7]

In the first case, *Maqbool Hussain*,[8] an immigrant from Pakistan, was detained by an immigration officer, after he had been granted indefinite leave to remain on the basis of a passport which did not belong to him. In the second case, *Bangoo*,[9] a group of immigrants who had entered the country using false passports were charged and convicted of conspiracy. The court also recommended their deportation. The immigrants appealed, arguing that they were ordinarily resident in the UK and were therefore immune from deportation. The Court of Appeal rejected this, saying that because they had entered by deception their stay in this country was void from the start. They were therefore illegal entrants.

The definition of illegal entry was not, however, to be restricted even to those who had entered by deception. It was to be widened to cover even those who had entered through the deception of a third party. Thus in 1977, the Court of Appeal held that Ijaz Begum Khan, a Pakistani woman, was an illegal entrant because she had entered on the passport of another person.[10] Ijaz Begum Khan was unable to read or write. When she came to Britain from Pakistan, her husband gave her his second wife's passport which she duly presented when she passed through immigration control. She had no reason to believe that she was involved in any fraud. Despite this, the Court of Appeal held in 1977 that she was an illegal entrant and as guilty as if she had organised the fraud herself.

One week after the Khan decision, the Court of Appeal made a ruling which, barrister Ian MacDonald has said, 'set the tone for all future cases'. The Court held that Safdar Hussain[11] was an illegal entrant because he had obtained indefinite leave to remain as a returning resident, either because he had used a false identity or had lied about his previous stay. This case, MacDonald says, not only decided that leave to enter obtained by deception was completely void. It decided also that questions of *fact* were matters for the Home Secretary to decide. The courts would not interfere if the Home Secretary acted in good faith and had reasonable grounds for concluding that the person detained was an illegal entrant.[12]

In the wake of such cases, the Home Secretary was forced to extend the 1974 amnesty to those who had entered by deception before 1973. Like the original amnesty, this was not automatic and many of those who did apply (178, or 28 per cent) were told that they were not eligible. In any case, the amnesty did not prevent the judges and the immigration authorities from continuing to widen the scope of the law, as we shall see in the next chapter. Moreover, the amnesties did not prevent a rapid rise in the number of people removed as illegal entrants. Thus in 1973, the first year of the Act's operation, only 80 people were removed. By 1976, when the Home Office redefinition of the law had become apparent, 270 were removed, rising to 490 in 1977. In the first five years of the Act, 1,100 people were removed as alleged illegal entrants.[13]

Overstaying occurs where someone who has been given leave to remain in the UK for a limited time remains beyond that period without having obtained an extension. This concept was also redefined to the detriment of many people lawfully in the country. Overstaying is a criminal offence which usually results in a fine and deportation. In the 1976 case of *Subramaniam*,[14] the Court of Appeal ruled that someone who had a limited leave to remain and who was refused an extension by the Home Office could appeal against the refusal only if they had applied for the extension before their initial limited leave expired. This was designed to stop the use of appeals to prolong a stay in the country. But in the same year the House of Lords went even further. In the case of *Suthendran*,[15] it ruled that there was a right of appeal against a refusal of an extension, but only where the application for extension and the Home Office decision were both made before the initial leave expired. The result was that people could apply for extensions, say two weeks before their initial leave expired, only to find that the Home Office took four weeks to deal with the application, by which time the initial leave had expired and, according to the House of Lords decision, they had no right of appeal. The House of Lords was fully aware of the effect of its decision, but said that the injustice could be dealt with by administrative means.

The decisions marked a change in policy, in that previously, applications for extensions which had been made out of time had in general been accepted in the normal way by the Home Office. In addition, the House of Lords decision meant that those applying for extensions now had to take into account, and could be jeopardised by, delays by the Home Office in dealing with their application.

As a result of the criticism which greeted the decisions, the government announced that all those who had applied for an extension before their initial leave had expired would be allowed an extra-statutory appeal. This was a temporary measure, and a more permanent arrangement was made the same year ensuring that anyone who applied for an extension before their leave expired would be given a period of 28 days after the Home Office decision in which to appeal.

## Law enforcement

Even before the Immigration Act came into force, a new national police unit concerned with immigration was set up within the Metropolitan Police. The Illegal Immigration Intelligence Unit (IIIU) based at New Scotland Yard in London was set up with a skeleton staff in September 1972 and became fully operational in March 1973 with a staff of ten police and one civilian. The function of the new unit, according to the Home Office, was to 'receive, collate, evaluate and disseminate information on known or *suspected* offenders'.[16] In practice, it is supposed to be informed whenever premises are to be searched for illegal entrants, whenever someone is arrested and found to be in possession of an identity card or passport believed to be forged, and whenever information is received regarding suspected illegal entrants.

The establishment of the IIIU was part of a more general reorganisation of 'C' department in the Metropolitan Police. According to the Metropolitan Police Commissioner's report for 1972, this was designed to 'place much greater emphasis on achieving an improved flow of intelligence and a better direction of effort against more worthwhile targets'. The Unit, which was set up without any reference to parliament and which is account-able only to the Commissioner and, through him, to the Home Secretary, was closely linked to another new unit set up at the same time, the Central Drugs Intelligence Unit. This linking of the two units was not coincidental. Official thinking had for some time made a close connection between the use of drugs and the presence of black people. The stereotype of the 'drug-taking black', usually West Indian, was common among police since the 1960s. In 1970, for instance, at a time when the Metropolitan Police CID had been given an extra 20 officers to deal with illegal immigration and drug trafficking, the Assistant Commissioner (Crime) Peter Brodie told the British Medical Association that the police found strong links between illegal immigration and drugs. Cannabis, he said, was used as tender to pay in whole or in part for the entry of illegal immigrants.[17] Brodie therefore managed to make a dual connection in one statement: black people were not only heavily involved in drugs, but were simul-taneously involved in drugs and illegal immigration, the one leading to the other.

In its first year of operation the IIIU carried out 219 enquiries concerning alleged illegal entrants, involving 73 arrests. This included the 'passport raids' in north London which are dealt with below. In his 1973 report, the Commissioner claimed: 'Some of this work attracted criticism but we make every effort to discharge responsibilities in a way which minimises the causes of friction between the immigrant community and the police'. In 1975, the number of enquiries carried out by the Unit had risen to 261 and the number of arrests to 95. In addition, the Commis-sioner reported that 'the volume of information collected and processed showed a significant increase'. By the following year, the Commissioner could report that, 'as expertise has been built up a greater awareness of the facilities afforded by the Unit has led to increased demand for its services from all parts of the country and from overseas'. This was to be the last reference by the Commissioner to the work of the Unit in his annual report and no further information has appeared in any report since.

The IIIU worked closely with the immigration service's own intelligence unit which had been set up in 1970. Based at Harmondsworth, near Heathrow airport (also the site of the main immigration detention centre), the unit was set up to collate, evaluate and circulate information on all aspects of the evasion of immigration control. It receives information from, and passes it to, other sections of the immigration service and also maintains close links with the police throughout the UK and with immigration services in other European countries.

As we saw, the Immigration Act increased police involvement in the enforcement of immigration control by giving officers extensive powers. Within months of the statute coming into force, the police took action using these new powers. On 11 October 1973 they raided 13 addresses in east London and questioned all those present about their immigration status. A number of people were taken to Leman Street police station, including one man who had been resident in Britain for six years.

Two weeks later, a further raid took place in Camden, north London, on 25 October. A rooming house with accomodation for 80 men was raided early in the morning by police and immigration officers. The men, all Asian, said that the police showed no warrants and were abusive. One man who was unable to produce his passport – because he had sent it to the Home Office – but who could produce the Home Office receipt as well as his employment voucher was taken to the police station and held for several hours before local police confirmed that they had checked his status three years previously and had found it in order.[18]

Despite protests from Camden Committee for Community Relations, Home Secretary Robert Carr turned down a request for a public inquiry into the incident on the grounds that such an inquiry would 'not result in any further substantial clarification of disputed facts' and it 'would not be possible for the police or the immigration service to disclose the precise information on which the operation was based'.

In December 1975 and in February 1976, there was a series of raids on clothing factories in east and south London. On 20 February, for example, the premises of Red Ten Fashions and Desilu Fashions were entered by 11 police officers and six immigration officers. One Bangladeshi worker was told by a police officer, 'You are here illegally', and was taken to the police station. After a few hours he was taken to his home and on showing the police his passport allowed to go free. In all, six people were detained, of whom only one was subsequently held as a seaman deserter. Those who were present during the raid were of the opinion that the search had no particular person in mind and that the operation was clearly a 'fishing expedition'.[19]

The most extensive raid of this period occurred in Newcastle-upon-Tyne in December 1977 when a number of Bangladeshi homes and restaurants were raided by police and immigration officers in search of four alleged illegal entrants and one seaman deserter. In a raid which began at 7 a.m. (a time justified by Home Office minister, Shirley Sumerskill, on the ground that this was 'thought likely to cause minimum disturbance to the business of the restaurants'[20]), 62 people were questioned, of whom 24 were detained because they were unable to satisfy immigration officers immediately that they were not in breach of immigration law. They were taken to the police station and most were released after varying periods of detention once they had established the legality of their stay. Seven of those detained were however transferred in handcuffs to the central police in Newcastle, and some were then held in Durham Prison. Three of them, having been detained in custody for several weeks, were eventually allowed to remain in the country, while three were deported.

Despite the fact that less than ten per cent of those questioned in the Newcastle raids were found to be in breach of immigration law, Home Office minister Shirley Sumerskill maintained that she would consider the idea of random raids 'repugnant and . . . potentially most damaging to the climate necessary for racial harmony'. The police and the immigration service had, however, she said, an obligation to enforce the law and do so with 'discretion' and a full awareness of the government's concern that 'no section of the community should be subjected to indiscriminate speculative investigations'.[21] Chapter 3 shows that such assurances meant little, since subsequent raids by the police and immigration service not only continued but increased in number and extent.

Passport raids were not the only way in which the policing of the Immigration Act was carried out. The police were also questioning individuals about their immigration status and demanding to see passports even where there was no reason to believe that any immigration offence had been committed. This practice has existed since immigration controls began, although it had always been official policy that it ought not to happen. In 1973, for example, the Home Office sent a circular to all chief constables asking them to avoid actions which could be construed as harassment of black people, for example, 'a request to inspect the passport of someone who comes to . . . notice in connection with a minor offence but whom there is no reason to suspect of being in the country illegally'.[22] In 1974, an instruction to this effect was written into the Metropolitan Police rule book.[23] Such advice and rules appeared to have little influence on police practice.

Only months after the Immigration Act came into force, the Pakistan Action Group said that it had monitored many cases where black motorists who had been stopped for minor road traffic offences were told to produce their passports.[24] In 1974 the magazine *Race Today* reported a number of cases where black people had been required to produce their passports. They included an East African Asian woman who had sought directions from a police officer and was then taken to a police station until her passport could be brought, and a party where all the (black) guests were told to produce their passports.[25] The police and the immigration service were not, however, the only people who were enforcing the immigration laws within Britain.

Internal controls were also operating in relation to work, both when people applied for a national insurance number and in the workplace itself. In 1970 an experiment was carried out at some local DHSS offices where first-time applicants for national insurance numbers were required to produce evidence of their identity to verify the details given in their application. In 1973, Sir Keith Joseph, then Secretary of State for Social Services, announced the general introduction of a procedure whereby those who held passports would be asked to produce them. He said that this would be to confirm the accuracy of personal particulars required for national insurance purposes, but if any irregularities were noticed which gave rise to suspicions of illegal entry or presence, then the Home Office would be informed.[26]

This procedure was introduced in 1975 and since then every applicant for a national insurance number has had to produce evidence of identity. In the case of citizens of the UK and the Irish Republic this means a passport or birth certificate, in the case of EEC nationals, a passport or official identity card, while all others must produce their passports. DHSS offices thus effectively became agents of immigration control, checking on the status of those seeking national insurance numbers and informing the Home Office of those whose status appears in some way to be irregular.

Even before the new procedure came into operation the police had been able to use the national insurance system in their enforcement of the immigration laws. As early as 1972, the *Times* reported one police officer saying that, 'If we know the name of a man we wish to find we get the Department [of Employment] to feed it into the computer to see if his address in the National Insurance records is thrown up'.[27]

At the same time, the checking of immigration status at the workplace itself also increased. As early as 1973, when the Immigration Act came into force, it was reported that checks of immigration status might take place. The *Daily Telegraph* reported that following the arrest by the Special Branch of a junior doctor in Southport who had overstayed, hospital authorities said that they might start checking the status of immigrant employees. In future, 'for their own peace of mind', the authorities would have to check on work permits.[28]

But sanction for the practice of checking passports and immigration status also came from the government itself. In 1976, Employment Minister John Golding said that people born outside the EEC were required to produce their passports or police registration certificates to show that they were eligible to take part in the government Training Opportunities Scheme, since the scheme required an undertaking that the trainee intended to work in the UK or the EEC on completion of training.

At the same time, Britain was coming under pressure from the EEC to establish a formal system of controls at the workplace and, in particular, to create a new criminal offence of taking or providing unlawful employment. Britain had joined the EEC in 1972 and had already discriminated against black people even as it did so. The Treaty of Accession to the Community signed on 22 January 1972 had two appendices, both of which were addressed to the question of black people and the right to freedom of movement which accession was supposed to bring.

The first appendix was a 'Joint Declaration on the Free Movement of Workers' by all the member states and the President of the Council of the European Communities. It said that the enlargement of the EEC could give rise to 'certain difficulties for the social situation' in one or more of the member states. They therefore reserved the right, 'should difficulties of that nature arise', to bring the matter before the institutions of the Community. Although the Joint Declaration did not mention race and colour, it was clearly aimed at black Britons. Both the Dutch and German governments were known to have expressed concern at the prospect of numbers of black Britons taking advantage of the free movement provisions and travelling to the Netherlands and Germany to look for work. The Dutch had at one point claimed that only those born in the EEC should be entitled to freedom of movement and in 1971 a Dutch Foreign Ministry official was quoted as saying: 'We think they [Commonwealth citizens] would come here because of our good social services.'[29]

The second appendix, which also discriminated, was the definition of British nationality for the purposes of EEC membership. This excluded from the definition of British national, and therefore from the freedom of movement provisions, Commonwealth citizens who, although not citizens of the UK and Colonies, were patrial because they had a patrial parent. At the time, this was reckoned to apply to the majority of Commonwealth citizens settled in the UK.[30] The definition also excluded UK passport-holders from East Africa who had not been in the UK for five years.

Four years later, in 1976, further discrimination against black people was threatened, this time from within the EEC itself. Although to date this pressure has not led to the creation of new offences or the establishment of a system of formal workplace controls, the episode illustrates what could happen and the extent of the pressure which could be brought to bear. It is therefore worth examining in some detail.

The Council of Ministers of the EEC adopted an 'Action Programme in favour of Migrant Workers and their Families' in February 1976 which specifically referred to the problems of illegal immigration and recommended various sanctions. Proposals to counter illegal immigration were prepared which would give employers a formal role in the enforcement of immigration controls, including fines on those who employed illegal immigrants. This met with strong opposition from the British government, which argued that there should be no binding directive since the question of illegal immigration in the UK was of a qualitatively different nature from that in other member states; the UK, as an island, had far more effective controls at points of entry than was possible in any of the other EEC states which shared common borders. In addition, the British government argued that to make employers assist in the directive's enforcement would lead to accusations of breaches of the race relations laws and might necessitate the introduction of identity cards.

Following such objections, a reconsidered draft directive was published by the Commission in November 1976. This proposed certain guidelines for the prevention and control of illegal immigration. These would be incorporated into the legislation of the individual member states. In particular, this version of the directive would have required states to provide: (1) intending immigrants before they left their home country with accurate information about living and working conditions and the law on entry and employment; (2) adequate controls at points of entry or at places of employment; (3) adequate control of employment agencies; (4) sanctions against those who knowingly organised or participated in activities leading to illegal immigration or illegal employment, including imprisonment and liability to the costs of repatriating illegal immigrants or workers. The most important change was the alternative offered to member states, of control either at the point of entry or at the workplace. The earlier draft had required both. In addition, the revised draft sought to impose sanctions on those who had knowingly participated in illegal immigration or employment, where the earlier version would have included even those who had taken part unwittingly.

The revised version of the draft directive was considered by the House of Lords Select Committee on the European Communities and its report was published in 1977.[31] The Committee repeated the argument that Britain had more effective controls on entry than was possible in the other member states and that, consequently, the estimated scale of illegal immigration in Britain was considerably smaller than in other countries. The controls implemented by the 1971 Immigration Act had, the Committee said, substantially met the requirements of the directive. Further, the Committee acknowledged, renewed public debate on illegal immigration would serve to increase the 'already sensitive and vulnerable position of black minorities in the United Kingdom'. On the specific question of workplace controls, the Select Committee said that these would be less effective and would involve undesirable administrative procedures, including 'elaborate arrangements for identification' with spot checks and 'other similar illiberal measures' which were 'especially deplored'.

The Labour government of the time said that it supported the broad aims behind the directive but accepted that they created a number of practical and legal problems. Home Office Minister, Shirley Sumerskill, told MPs in June 1977 that she was sure that it was right, especially at a time of high unemployment, 'to do all we can to deal with people who entered the country illegally or took work in breach of conditions'. Employment Minister John Grant, however, said that he had made it clear on a number of occasions to the EEC Council of Ministers that there was 'no question of our taking any action which could undermine our race relations legislation and give rise to the charge that we were engaging in a witch hunt'. The minister also quashed suggestions that the Factory Inspectorate or the Wages Councils might be used to enforce the provisions of the directive. It was 'inconceivable', he said, that the Factory Inspectorate would be used in this way and 'impractical' to use the Wages Councils.

Yet another revised draft directive was published in April 1978 which was even wider in scope than the previous version. It defined illegal immigration and employment not by reference to 'the national legislation regulating such matters' (as the earlier draft had done), but by reference to 'law, regulation or administrative action', thus covering virtually any decision by the relevant authorities. The revised draft also appeared to have taken little or no account of the objections made by the British government, for it still required member states to organise 'adequate controls, especially of employers and persons and undertakings supplying manpower to third parties' and it still required the application of serious sanctions on those involved in illegal immigration and employment.

This time the draft directive was considered by the House of Commons Select Committee on European Legislation which reported that the directive raised questions of 'legal and political importance' and recommended further consideration by parliament. It pointed out that the revised text retained the very proposals which had been criticised by members of the UK parliament.

Outside parliament too there was extensive criticism of the revised directive. The Commission for Racial Equality, giving evidence to the parliamentary Select Committee on Race Relations and Immigration inquiry into the effects of EEC membership, said that the directive might have the:

> unintended and undesirable effect of discouraging employers from employing people from the minority communities. It is possible . . . that, with additional checks in the employment field, some employers will say, 'We are not going to lay ourselves open to this sort of scrutiny and business and argument and so forth. We will take the easy way out; we will not risk it; we will employ fewer members of the minority communities'.[32]

The Migrants' Action Group said that the introduction of criminal sanctions against employers would encourage them to refuse work to migrants and immigrants on the ground that they might be illegal entrants, even if, in fact, the real reason was racial discrimination. Checks at workplaces would require the 'unacceptable' introduction of some sort of identity card system, a point also made by the Joint Council for the Welfare of Immigrants which said that implementation of the proposal would, in effect, require all workers to carry identification papers. Though even this could hardly be expected to help since identity cards were already necessary in the countries which supported the draft directive.

Despite such criticism, the draft directive was debated and passed by the European parliament in October 1978. Speaking in the debate, British Conservative MEP Elaine Kellett-Bowman promised that a future Conservative government in the UK would set up an inquiry to investigate ways of controlling illegal immigration and overstaying. The present directive, however, would 'place a grave strain on race relations' and could be interpreted 'to mean the necessity of police raids on factories, in which dark-skinned or black immigrants would inevitably be the focus of attention'.[33] The European parliament nevertheless passed the directive with only minor amendments. Yet when the European Commission's social affairs council discussed the matter the following month, it took no action to approve the directive as Community law, presumably because of the strength of British opposition.

The European Commission was also probably aware of the developments taking place in Britain in response to the report of the Select Committee on Race Relations and Immigration on internal controls. It would have been aware, for example, that in July 1978 the government said it would 'continue to give a high priority in the allocation of resources to the prevention of abuse and evasion of immigration control' and that improved liaison between the agencies involved, together with the development of the immigration service computer, would greatly increase the effectiveness of immigration control. In other words, it might well have been convinced that as far as Britain was concerned there was no need for further measures.

The question of illegal immigration was not, however, forgotten, and in 1979 the EEC Commission returned to the subject in a discussion document on the harmonisation of member states' policies on immigration from countries outside the EEC.[34] As yet, however, there have been no formal attempts either to resuscitate the 1978 directive, or to formulate other plans for dealing with illegal immigration and unauthorised employment which would involve the establishment of formal workplace controls and sanctions. Nevertheless, the directive is important because it shows clearly what *can* happen and what pressures can be brought to bear, and because it illustrates the need for concerted opposition in such circumstances. In this context it is worth noting that the response in Britain to the question of formal workplace controls was not uniformly critical. The Hotel and Catering Industry Committee of the Trades Union Congress, for example, expressed its agreement with the 1978 Select Committee's recommendation that the police and other agencies should be given substantially more resources to trace overstayers and tackle all other aspects of illegal immigration, including unauthorised working. It further agreed to inform the Home Secretary that his proposal for using the national insurance scheme to identify people who needed authority to work was 'worthy of further consideration, and that more resources should be provided to improve enforcement'.[35] The Committee subsequently decided, reportedly under pressure from the TUC's Equal Rights Committee, that while the problem of unauthorised working within the catering trades could not be ignored, any effective means of enforcing the law could well exacerbate community relations and lead to 'unacceptable levels of surveillance'. The problem, it accepted, had therefore to be tackled in a 'more positive fashion' involving greater organisational efforts by the unions and better policing of the minimum wage levels by the Wages Councils.[36] But the earlier support from the Hotel and Catering Industry Committee showed that there was considerable support for formal workplace controls within the trade union movement, specifically from a section where migrant workers formed a significant part of the labour force.

In other areas, too, during this period, internal controls were developing. In 1974, for example, it was reported that Ealing Education Authority had been asking the parents of black children to produce their passports before the children were taken on to the school register. At the time Ealing was still bussing black children to schools outside their immediate areas so as to ensure that no more than one third of pupils in a school were black, and there may well have been some connection.[37] The council claimed that they were simply collecting data for surveys conducted by the Department of Education.[38]

In the health service black people found themselves challenged about their eligbility for NHS treatment. Nearly 200 Asian women attending the Leicester General Hospital's ante-natal clinics in 1976 were asked to produce their passports before receiving care. One woman who had previously given birth to a child at the hospital refused to do so and was subsequently refused ante-natal care. The matter was then taken up in parliament by the Liberal peer, Lord Avebury.

Under the National Health Service Act of 1948, free health care was supposed to be available to 'the people of England and Wales' (and under separate legislation, 'the people of Scotland'). The Department of Health and Social Security had come to interpret this phrase as meaning those who were 'ordinarily resident' in the country. Thus, it was not restricted to those who were citizens of the United Kingdom and Colonies or even to them and to citizens of independent Commonwealth countries, but included work permit holders and students, and generally all those people staying in the country for prolonged periods.

When confronted with the case of the Asian women in Leicester, the then health minister Dr David Owen agreed that the practice:

> was open to objection in that it singles out one particular
> group in the community – those with foreign-sounding names
> – and apparently requires them as a matter of routine, to
> produce proof of eligibility to use the National Health Service
> every time they seek admission for non-emergency treatment.
> No other section of the public is expected to do this as a matter
> of routine, and the National Health Service is therefore open
> to the criticism that it discriminates . . . I really feel that I can't
> defend it.[39]

The practice of demanding passports from black people was therefore supposed to have been stopped. Shortly afterwards, however, another form of internal control in the health service came to light. In September 1976, a three-year-old Turkish boy suffering from leukaemia was turned away from St Bartholomew's Hospital in London because his parents were unable to guarantee meeting the cost of treatment. It was only after the intervention of Lord Brockway that the Department of Health and Social Security agreed to provide free treatment. As Lord Brockway said, the principle at stake was whether someone who was welcomed here on a work permit and who had contributed through taxes and national insurance contributions to the welfare state should have a right to free treatment for his son who had joined him here. The DHSS decision, however, did not establish a principle as it was clear that treatment in this case was being given only as an exception.[40] As we shall see in Chapter 4 the DHSS itself began to tighten up on the use of the health service, thus opening the way for even more checks and demands for passports.

## Conclusion

The early years after the Immigration Act 1971 was passed showed clearly that internal controls were to be an important part of the operation of the law. The Act, as passed by parliament, was racist in effect and intention, and the powers it bestowed on immigration officials and police were extensive. But even this wide framework was to have its boundaries extended in a quite unforeseen development. The courts, far from acting as a so-called bulwark between the state and the citizen, actually strengthened the powers of the government to the extreme detriment of the – black – individual. The racism institutionalised by law in the Immigration Act was affirmed and refined by the judges. In doing so, they brought within the scope of the criminal law many people who had previously had no reason to fear that they were in any way in breach of the law. The security of a whole community began to be undermined.

Government ministers are fond of saying that it is the function of the courts to interpret the law and that they are not responsible for what the courts decide. But this suggests that cases somehow reach the courts of their own accord, when, of course, they have to be brought there in the first place. Immigration cases have always reached the courts because of Home Office practice. Had the Home Office not decided to allege, for example, that Azam and his two co-accused were covered by the Immigration Act, even though they had entered the country before it came into effect, the court could not have made the ruling which it did. In fact the Home Office bears an enormous responsibility for the interpretation of the immigration laws which occurred in this period.

Between them, the Home Office and the courts set the tone for the enforcement of immigration laws. The police and the immigration service, both of whom laid their plans even before the Act came into effect, began, through passport raids and checks, the kind of policing which they intended to continue.

But the climate of suspicion which the Home Office and the courts had helped to create, also served to encourage others to carry out their own enforcement of the immigration laws. Employers, hospitals and schools began their own checking of black people and in so doing paved the way for one of the most insidious developments in internal control, a development which is looked at in more detail in Chapter 4.

Although concern was voiced at these developments, from black people themselves, the occasional community relations council and others, most of the anxiety about the immigration laws still focused on the question of control on entry – the delays in processing applications for entry clearance, the refusal of immigration officials to believe the evidence before them, the refusal of entry at ports, the detention and imprisonment of immigrants and so on. What was happening *inside* Britain to the settled black community was largely ignored.

The developments described in this chapter, which were to pave the way for the extension of internal controls, happened, it should not be forgotten, under both Conservative and Labour governments, and black people experienced little difference between the immigration laws of one and the other. The Tories may have been responsible for enacting the legislation, but Labour did nothing to repeal it. Labour did announce an amnesty for those affected by some of the court decisions, but many applications were turned down and in any case, the amnesties did nothing to stop either the further widening of the law or the further development of internal control. The two parties shared the belief that immigration control was good for race relations and they vied with each other on who could implement it most effectively.

# 3. The system takes shape

Two crucial factors in the development of internal immigration controls in Britain appeared in 1978. The first was the emergence of a radical new Tory philosophy on racism and immigration which would play a large part in sweeping the party into office during the following year. The second was the publication of the report of the parliamentary Select Committee on Race Relations and Immigration which called unanimously for a government inquiry into the establishment of a system of internal control.[1] To understand these developments properly it is necessary at this point to trace their origins.

Ever since controls on the immigration of people from the Commonwealth began in 1962, British immigration policy was based on what came to be known as the 'numbers game': the idea that fewer black people made for better race relations. In effect, this defined the 'problem' as the presence of black people, not the response of white people to black people. The solution to the problem was therefore obvious: control of the black presence. Once the numbers game was started it could not be stopped, for it contained within it a compelling racist logic. The point has been expressed cogently in Robert Moore's book, *Racism and Black Resistance in Britain:*

> Once the debate is about numbers there are no issues of principle to be discussed *only how many?* . . . The argument about numbers is unwinnable because however many you decide upon there will always be someone to campaign for less and others for whom one is too many. Since you have admitted that black people are a problem in themselves, it is impossible to resist the argument for less of them.[2]

As Moore, pointed out, even if new 'primary' immigration were stopped altogether, the argument could be shifted to the question of dependants. Even if the number of dependants were reduced, the argument could shift to the issue of illegal immigration and allegations that the statistics were wrong. In the last analysis, Moore wrote, 'if you play the numbers game then black people already here and every black child born here is a problem and the discussion shifts to questions of deportation'.[3]

This is precisely what has happened. As we have seen, the 1971 Immigration Act virtually ended black 'primary' immigration, largely restricting future immigration to the dependants of those already settled in Britain. But this did not mean an end to the great 'immigration debate'. Instead, it further encouraged those who wished to see the numbers of black people reduced even more by virtually any means available. Shortly after the Act was passed Britain witnessed a resurgence of the openly fascist right whose organisational basis was – and remains – anti-black racism and whose main policy was an end to immigration and the repatriation, by force if necessary, of all black people in the UK.

But this preoccupation with immigration and the numbers game was not to be found only on the margins of British politics. Centre stage, the scenario which Moore had anticipated had unfolded. In 1976, for example, in a widely reported speech, Enoch Powell quoted extensively from an unpublished report of a visit to the Indian sub-continent by D.F. Hawley, a senior Foreign Office official. Hawley had been asked to examine immigration procedures in the sub-continent, particularly the methods for screening dependants. His report claimed that while genuine dependants were being treated by immigration authorities as satisfactorily as possible, an increasing number were gaining entry fraudulently. It was alleged that the 'concession' made by the Labour government over the admission of husbands and fiancés was being abused. Not only this, but the so-called concession involved a 'multiplier factor' since it also entitled the parents, grandparents and other distressed relatives of the fiancé to apply for entry. The 'problem', Hawley added, was not finite, since the number of dependants had never accurately been computed.

The Labour government's response was predictable, managing in the one breath to state that Hawley had got his facts wrong and to assure that the actual numbers of people coming in – or waiting to – were not that great. Two months after Powell's speech, Home Secretary Roy Jenkins announced that a special committee chaired by Lord Franks would examine 'the possibility and usefulness of a register of dependants of those settled in this country, who are entitled or have a claim under the immigration laws to join them here'. Franks reported in February 1977, neither recommending nor rejecting the idea of a register but offering a consideration of the arguments, practical issues and likely effects involved.

Jenkins' successor at the Home Office, Merlyn Rees, announced that the government had decided that a register would not be desirable or practicable. At the same time, he assured the public, firm action would be taken to check abuses of the present system, including new immigration rules to deal with 'marriages of convenience' aimed solely at achieving entry or avoiding removal. The rule changes followed in March. They provided that husbands would be allowed entry only for an initial period of 12 months (unless the marriage was more than one year old). Leave to remain after this 'probationary' period would not be granted if the Home Secretary had reason to believe that the marriage was one of convenience. In order to discover whether marriages were genuine, couples were subjected to interrogations about their sleeping arrangements and birth control practices, as well as repeated visits by immigration or police officers to confirm cohabitation.

A few months later, the Central Policy Review Staff published a report on British representation overseas, including the administration of immigration control abroad. The Think Tank recommended a relaxation of certain controls abroad, and the tightening up of internal controls within the UK. Like the Select Committee report which was to follow the next year, the Central Policy Review Staff recommended a government inquiry into the creation of a formal system of internal control.[4] The Select Committee had already announced in 1976 that its next inquiry would be into 'the assumptions made by the Government about potential immigration' and related matters, although the inquiry did not get under way until 1977. Its report, as we have already seen, was published in March the following year, but before Tory thinking about immigration had become clear.

There had been indications in the press that a Tory 'rethink' on immigration was in progress: junior home affairs spokesman Keith Speed was said to have been asked to prepare detailed policy plans for reducing immigration to be put to the Shadow Cabinet by Easter. Then in a television interview on 30 January, 1978, in her first public statement on the subject for nearly a year, Margaret Thatcher indicated which way the wind was blowing. The British people, she claimed, were afraid that they might be 'rather swamped by people with a different culture'. The Tories would hold out the prospect of a clear end to immigration.

Two months later, at the annual meeting of the Central Council of the Conservative Party in Leicester, William Whitelaw spelled out what this would mean in practice. The aim of the policy, he said, was 'to introduce certainty and finality into our plans so that we can end the constant and widespread preoccupation with levels of immigration and so the anxieties of our people about them'. To this end the Tories would implement a new law on nationality; parents, grandparents and children over 18 of those already here would be admitted only if they fulfilled stringent conditions for distressed relatives; the husbands and fiancés of women in the UK would be allowed in only 'if an exceptional degree of hardship would result' from the woman being required to live abroad; work permits would be reduced to the absolute minimum and the practice of removing restrictions after four years in approved employment would be ended; a register of dependants would be created; and an inquiry would be set up to consider a system of internal control.

The Tories and the Select Committee had more in common than just the general substance of their proposals. The ideology behind their respective recommendations was also of a piece. When the Tories jettisoned the then bi-partisan policy on immigration, they did so not just to win back the voters which they knew they were losing to the National Front, but also because the dominant ideology within the party had shifted from a belief that immigration control was good for race relations (this was, after all, shared with Labour): they now argued that immigration control had become necessary to protect the 'British way of life'.

The Select Committee had also made it clear that what they had in mind was necessary to preserve the British way of life. For example, on the question of arranged marriages it said 'we believe that the members of these [ethnic] minorities should themselves pay greater regard to the *mores* of their country of adoption and, indeed, also to their own traditional pattern of the bride joining the husband's family'.[5] And on the question of the admission of dependent children, the Committee said that to spare them the 'traumatic experience of being admitted totally unprepared' for the British education and teenage society, 'it may well be necessary on social grounds to adjust the Immigration Rules in the future to ensure children are only admitted if they are below school age'.[6] As Sivanandan commented at the time, what the Select Committee appeared to be saying was, 'If you are here, be like us, if you cannot, go home'.[7]

For its part, Labour was quick to reject the Select Committee recommendations (although, as we have seen, Labour MPs had supported them) and to appeal pathetically for race and immigration issues to be removed from the party political arena and to seek an all-party approach. The Labour government had rejected the idea of an inquiry into a system of internal control and it also rejected the recommendation that only children up to the age of 12 be admitted as dependants. At the same time, it assured the public that black immigration was falling and that there would be no further major primary immigration in the foreseeable future. The police and the immigration service would maintain their efforts to detect illegal immigrants; an inquiry into overstaying announced in 1977 would continue, as would plans for the immigration service computer facilities. The level of enforcement had evidently already risen: the number of deportation orders made, and the number of illegal entrants detected and removed were two to three times higher in 1977 than in 1973. The Labour government promised it would continue to give a high priority in the allocation of resources to the prevention of abuse and the evasion of immigration control, developing the effectiveness of information gathering and improving liaison between the agencies involved.

Although the Select Committee report and recommendations were rejected, they succeeded in putting the government on the defensive and, equally important, in shifting the terms of immigration control even further than they had gone before. (The mere fact that a report like this could emerge, unanimously, from a bi-partisan committee spoke volumes about the level of British racism.)

Internal controls were more firmly on the agenda than ever before, as the Home Office, the courts, the police and the immigration service would quickly show. Initially, such controls would be implemented by Labour, but waiting in the wings to put the spirit, if not the letter, of the Select Committee proposals into effect when the opportunity arose, was a Conservative Party which shared its assumptions and philosophy.

## The judges' role

The redefinition of the law begun in the early years of the Immigration Act continued into the late 1970s and 1980s. In 1979, for example, the Divisional Court ruled that a work permit holder was an illegal entrant because she had not disclosed that she had dependent children.[8] Mrs Claveria had obtained a work permit in 1973 to work as a resident domestic. At the time, such permits were only granted to people without children. In 1976, Mrs Claveria returned to the Philippines for a holiday and married. The following year, she completed her four years in approved employment and had all the conditions on her stay removed. She then applied for her husband to join her and he was granted a visa. On his arrival in the UK he was questioned by immigration officers who discovered that Mrs Claveria had three children at the time of her original entry to the UK in 1973. Mr Claveria was refused entry on the ground that his wife was an illegal entrant, and following the Divisional Court ruling in 1979, Mrs Claveria herself was removed from the UK.

The *Claveria* ruling put nearly 300 people at risk, merely because they too had children when they obtained their work permits. In many cases, the workers themselves had practised no deception since the work permits had been obtained by employment agencies. Indeed, the Home Office accepted that the agencies were often responsible for any deception practised, but nevertheless refused to make any general concession. A further 100 migrant workers were alleged by the Home Office to be illegal entrants because, it was alleged, they had submitted false references in support of applications for work permits. Again, in many cases, employment agencies, and not the workers themselves, had obtained the permits and it was therefore the agencies who were guilty of any deception. In both cases, only a determined and long-running struggle by the Resident Domestics' Campaign prevented the removal of almost three quarters of those threatened as illegal entrants. And it would seem that the Department of Employment and the Home Office were both aware of the alleged deception long before they decided to take any action. Before 1978, for example, women who had completed four years in employment were allowed to be joined by their dependent children.

In the same year as the Divisional Court ruling on the Claveria case, Erlinda Suboc was told by an immigration adjudicator that she was an illegal entrant because she had not disclosed the fact that she was pregnant, even though she had already tried to abort and was hoping to obtain an abortion in the UK.[9]

The reinterpretation of illegal entry reached its furthest point in 1980 with the House of Lords ruling in the case of *Zamir*. Zamir was 15 when an application was made on his behalf for him to join his father in the UK. The application stated that he was unmarried. The immigration authorities took three years to deal with the application and when Zamir was eventually given a visa he was 18. The change in age was significant for a son over 18 could only claim to be a dependant and therefore entitled to entry into the UK if he was unmarried. After receiving the visa but before travelling to the UK, Zamir married. Technically this meant that he was no longer entitled to join his father as a dependant.

Zamir travelled alone to the UK. His wife remained in Pakistan intending to join her husband at a later stage. Zamir passed through immigration control but was not questioned about his marital status. Two years later he applied for his wife to join him. He was interviewed and arrested as an illegal entrant, since his marriage had withdrawn his entitlement to entry as a dependant.

The Home Office never proved that Zamir knew of the significance of his marriage but this turned out to be irrelevant, for the House of Lords ruled that Zamir, and any immigrant, had to disclose to the immigration officer any change 'he knew or ought to have known' was material. An immigrant, Lord Wilberforce said, owed a 'positive duty of candour' on all material facts which denoted a change of circumstances since entry clearance was granted. The immigrant after all, he said, was 'seeking a privilege'.

The Zamir ruling was extensively criticised in legal journals and elsewhere but neither such criticism, nor an application to the European Commission on Human Rights, could prevent Zamir's deportation. It did play a part, however, in persuading the House of Lords to revise its own ruling within the relatively short period of three years in the cases of *Khera* and *Khawaja*, which are discussed on the following page. In the meantime, however, large numbers of people, often long established in the UK, continued to be removed from the UK as illegal entrants.

Alongside the judicial redefinition and widening of the scope of the meaning of 'illegal entry', there was a corresponding erosion of the one remedy available to alleged illegal entrants, that of *habeas corpus*. This is an ancient writ which requires a person detaining another to justify the detention before a court. As Andrew Nicol notes, the remedy has been the boast of English constitutional lawyers for generations and to the eminent Victorian constitutional writer, A.V. Dicey, 'for practical purposes it was worth a hundred constitutional articles guaranteeing individual liberty'.[10]

Under the Commonwealth Immigrants Acts the courts adopted an interpretation in *habeas corpus* applications which was strict in its attitude towards the authorities. In 1969, for example, 11 Pakistanis were found wandering in Surrey with wet clothes and sand in their shoes. They were detained and sought *habeas corpus*. The Home Secretary was unable to convince the court that the men had been apprehended within 24 hours of their arrival as laid down in the Commonwealth Immigrants Act 1962, and the court, accepting that there could have been explanations for the wetness and sand other than 'beach-sneaking'.

ordered the men's release. Later court decisions were not to take such a libertarian view.

In the 1978 case of *Safdar Hussain*, referred to in Chapter 2, the court refused to enquire into the relevant facts saying that it was sufficient if the Home Secretary had reasonable grounds for his belief. In the case of *Choudhary*, in the same year, the court added that the burden of proof in *habeas corpus* cases lay on the applicant and not, as had been held in previous cases, on the person detaining. Such decisions received the approval of the House of Lords in the case of *Zamir* in 1980 where it was stated 'without argument or qualification that it was for an applicant for *habeas corpus* to show that his or her detention was unlawful'.[11]

The considerable criticism levelled at the judgement in *Zamir* no doubt influenced the House of Lords to review the decision within the relatively short period of three years. Barrister Ian MacDonald has suggested that the House of Lords was also being responsive to a new mood or new power in the black community as shown most dramatically in the riots of 1981.

In the cases of *Khera* and *Khawaja* heard in 1983, the House of Lords did not dispute earlier rulings that entry by deception was illegal. However, it rejected the idea, laid down in *Zamir*, that immigrants had a 'positive duty of candour'. Mere non-disclosure of material facts did not, the Lords said, mean that entry was in breach of the immigration laws, provided that there was no fraud involved. In addition, the House of Lords re-affirmed that in *habeas corpus* applications the burden of proof lay on the authorities who had to justify the detention of someone as an illegal entrant, proving its case on the balance of probabilities.

The 1983 ruling was of considerable significance, but it left untouched much of the development in the law which had taken place since 1973. In any case, welcome though it was, it came too late to stop the removals of people held to have been illegal entrants which had risen to their highest level in the year of the *Zamir* ruling. In 1979, the year before the *Zamir* ruling, the number of alleged illegal entrants who were removed reached an all-time high of 590; but in 1980, the number rose by over 300 to

910. Between 1978 and 1982, 3,290 people were removed from the UK as alleged illegal entrants.[12]

The widening of the scope of the law was not, however, confined to the question of illegal entry. The Home Office also began to extend the circumstances in which it was prepared to order deportation on the ground that this was 'conducive to the pubilc good'. This power was normally used to order the deportation of someone who had been convicted, but not been recommended for deportation, by a court. Indeed, the immigration rules in force between 1973 and 1980 said that most of the deportations on 'conducive' grounds were of this kind. This remark was dropped from the 1983 rules, by which time it had become common for the Home Office to order deportation on 'conducive to the public good' grounds where it believed there had been a 'marriage of convenience'. Once again the courts upheld the Home Office practice and in January 1983, the Court of Appeal ruled that marriages of convenience were not conducive to the public good and that non-patrial spouses were liable to deportation.[13]

## New technology

While the courts were reinterpreting and extending the range of the law, the agencies responsible for its enforcement in practice, the police and the immigration service, were increasing in number and expanding their resources.

By 1980, for instance, the Metropolitan Police Illegal Immigration Intelligence Unit had more than doubled its original size and comprised 24 police officers and two civilians. The immigration service's own Intelligence Unit now had 31 officers and eight civilian staff, at an annual cost of £335,000.[14] But the increase in resources was not confined to personnel. The IIIU also benefited considerably from the development of the Metropolitan Police 'C' Department computer which came into operation in 1979, although planning had begun in 1973, only months after the IIIU had started operating.

The computer system is controversial on a number of grounds. It contains not only objective information such as names, addresses and physical descriptions, but also intelligence material consisting of the suppositions and suspicions of officers in the Unit. Neither the police nor the Home Office have divulged much information about the computer system: when it was being developed, police officials refused to answer questions put to them by journalists from the *Times* on the ground that to do so would constitute a breach of security, and the Home Secretary, Merlyn Rees, refused to provide information to parliament. Even the government-appointed Committee on Data Protection under Sir Norman Lindop was kept ignorant of the system, forcing it to the conclusion that:

> While we have no reason to believe that the public need be unduly alarmed by the general use of computers for police purposes, in relation to the Metropolitan Police we do not have enough evidence to give a firm assurance to that effect for all aspects of such use by them. [15]

When the specifications for the 'C' Department computer were drawn up in 1974 there were estimated to be around 13,000 names on the records then held by the IIIU. The specifications estimated a growth of around 360 records each month with an estimated total of 60,500 records by early 1985. In terms of the number of enquiries made of the computer, the specifications estimated 80 per month in 1974, rising to 370 each month by 1985. [16]

The immigration service Intelligence Unit also took advantage of this new technology of surveillance. In 1981 it installed a minicomputer at its headquarters in Harmondsworth to automate the tasks of surveillance, information gathering and supplying information to the police, in particular by computerising the Central Intelligence Index. This index includes details of those served with notice of further examination who leave the UK before consideration of their case is complete; those removed as illegal entrants; or following refusal of leave to enter, those refused entry clearances; and those who abscond before completion of their examination. According to the government, all data held on the computer are deleted after seven years. The government admitted that it was not possible to state precisely what evidence of abuse or attempted abuse of the immigration laws was required before a suspect was entered on the computer.

Much, it said, 'depends upon the source and the apparent reliability of the information'.[17]

About 300,000 names can be stored on the immigration service computer, which uses a programme called 'Status', described as a 'powerful tool for searching free text information . . . It permits data to be entered in free form text and any part of that text is accessed by entering key words'.[18] For example, workplace raids may result in arrests, since the status of suspected persons can be checked quickly either on the 'wanted/missing persons' index of the Police National Computer, which includes a list of people who 'may be illegally in the country', or on the immigration service computer after police have informed immigration staff of their names.

Even the names of people who are in Britain legally could be thrown up in such a search of the computer if they have appeared in the address book or other documents of someone who appears in the names index. As *Computing* noted:

> By using Status an immigration officer working at a terminal could go through a whole address book within minutes to check whether any names, addresses or telephone numbers appear in the databank. He could at the same time enter the address book into the databank. The software provides almost unlimited capacity to browse through information . . .[19]

It was precisely this kind of 'free text retrieval' or browsing through information in the hope of coming up with something, which gave the official Lindop Committee on Data Protection such cause for concern. The committee was clearly worried at the development of free text retrieval systems which allowed users to retrieve every incidence of particular items of information from a larger mass, and to discover the relationship of one piece of information to another. Such systems, the committee noted, 'are well suited to surveillance requirements'. As such, the committee concluded, they presented 'special problems . . . of control'.[20]

Although only immigration officials have direct access to the Harmondsworth computer, police forces throughout the UK can ring the Unit and request details of anyone they may suspect as an illegal entrant. As *Computing* concluded in its account of the new computer system, 'Since August 1981, such checks have become infinitely easier to perform'.[21]

While these specialist intelligence units were implementing the use of new technology, the Home Office announced in 1979 that the matching of landing and embarkation cards, which had previously been done manually, was to be computerised. Ever since the Aliens Act of 1905, people subject to immigration control have had to supply immigration officials with personal details, so that checks can be carried out on those entering and leaving the country. Under the 1971 Act anyone who is not a citizen of the UK or another EEC country has to complete a card on arrival and one on departure. Landing and embarkation cards are used in part to check that visitors to the UK do not stay beyond their allotted time. In cases where it appears that someone may have overstayed, enquiries will be initiated by the special overstayers tracing unit of the Immigration and Nationality Department.

The plans for computerising this process followed the special survey into overstaying which had been set up by the government in 1977, the year the Select Committee began its inquiry into immigration. This ended two years later, having, in the words of the Home Secretary, 'run into serious difficulties'.[22] The problems in matching accurately the large number of cards involved made it impossible to arrive at acceptable estimates of overstaying. But this did not prevent the Home Secretary from claiming that there was reason to be 'concerned about the effectiveness of our present measures' and that overstaying occurred to an extent which justified the 'further development of means to tackle it'. Effective post-entry measures were necessary, the Home Secretary said, and to the extent that its resources allowed, the Home Office and the immigration service were improving the means of following up cases with the co-operation of the police.

The most important 'further development' in this area – computerising the matching of landing and embarkation cards – began preliminary operation in May 1980. Full operation of the system began three months later at a cost of £140,000, with annual running costs of a further £140,000. The Home Secretary told parliament that the purpose of the computer was to indicate when someone had remained in the UK after his or her permitted stay. Information on arrivals at ports of entry, including name and other 'identifying particulars' along with conditions of stay, including time limit imposed on arrival, is passed to the Immigration and Nationality Department (IND) at Croydon. These data are then entered on computer terminals linked by telephone to the Home Office Automated Data Processing Unit (ADPU) at Bootle on Merseyside.

Any variation of conditions attached to stay – for example an extension of the permitted period of stay – is similarly fed into the computer from the IND at Croydon. The ADPU at Bootle in turn informs the IND if it does not receive notice of an embarkation card when the visitor's time has expired. The IND then puts in motion the physical process of tracing and apprehending the overstayer. If this proves unsuccessful the police are informed (through G11 division of the Metropolitan Police which is responsible for the Aliens Registration Office). The information is then placed on the Wanted and Missing Persons Index of the Police National Computer at Hendon, north London.

Initially, the computerisation of landing and embarkation cards was to handle about half a million arrivals and departures every year, although it is designed for further expansion. This means that the immigration service have to decide who is to be checked by computer since there are many more arrivals than can be handled by the system. In reply to parliamentary questions the government has said that people were more likely to be checked if they were admitted on a longer term basis, for example as students or for employment, than if they were admitted for short periods as visitors. The government declined, however, to provide details of which nationalities were primarily represented on the computer.[23]

The overstayers computer system was not an isolated development but the first part of a programme known as the Immigration and Nationality Department Electronic Computer System or INDECS. The second phase of INDECS, yet to be implemented, will automate the process further. Landing and embarkation cards will be replaced by computer terminals at ports which will automatically register those people who are given permission to be in Britain for a limited period only. The terminals will be linked to minicomputers which will in turn be linked to the main computer in Bootle. The system will therefore phase out cards altogether, replacing them with electronic signals with little need for any manual, human intervention.[24]

This second phase will also involve computerising the Home Office suspect index and the development of the computerised, machine-readable passport which is to be introduced in 1986. This aspect of the system is looked at in Chapter 5.

**Random investigations**

The practical policing of the immigration laws continued with renewed intensity. In January 1978, only one week after Home Office minister Dr Shirley Sumerskill had written to JCWI saying that the police enforced the law with 'discretion', a number of restaurants and snack bars in London's West End were visited by police and immigration officers. They detained for questioning some 40 people, mainly of middle eastern origin. Eleven of these were subsequently charged with offences under the Immigration Act.[25]

In March, two restaurants in Soho were raided and all the Chinese and Indian workers questioned. One man was detained overnight and only released early the next day because a friend brought his passport to the police station. In June, four restaurants and one house in varying areas of London were raided. Police and immigration officers questioned 18 people about their immigration status. Two people were detained, one for two and a half hours, the other for one hour, before being released. Only one person was charged with overstaying, despite a claim that the police were acting on information 'which appeared to come from a reliable source . . . that illegal immigrants were being harboured at these premises'.[26] In October 1978, police broke down the doors of an Indian restaurant in west London. The owner, his family and the restaurant workers, all of whom were sleeping on the premises, were required to produce their passports.[27]

The Home Office again denied that random raids were taking place. In response to protests from Camden Committee for Community Relations, Home Office minister Brynmor John said that he was 'very much opposed to "fishing expeditions"' and that he had been assured by the Metropolitan Police Commissioner that no operation which could be described in this way or as a 'blanket raid' was authorised.[28]

On 13 May 1980, a number of shops and other premises belonging to the Bestways chain in London were raided by 26 police and 19 immigration officers. Thirty-seven people were detained on suspicion of immigration law offences, including some who actually produced their passports when they were taken to their homes by the police. Of the 37, only nine were charged with an immigration offence. The remainder, including nine people who were patrial and therefore in theory not even subject to immigration control, were held by the police for varying periods of one to eight hours. One man who had been living in Britain for 22 years was held for seven hours. All those detained were denied access to solicitors and in one case, the home of a young Asian was unlawfully searched without a warrant and left ransacked. Those detained were given an opportunity to collect and produce documents proving the legality of their presence in the country only *after* they had been taken to the police station. In one case, no attempt was made to verify the information given by a man who quoted the number of his certificate of registration as a United Kingdom citizen. If it had been, his detention could have been avoided.

Less than two weeks later, another major raid took place at the Hilton Hotel in Park Lane. This involved questioning over 100 workers by 60 police and 16 immigration officers. Thirty-five of those questioned were detained, including two patrials and two non-patrials who were detained for several hours before establishing their right to be in Britain.

A third major raid was carried out at the Main Gas factory in north London in June 1980 and involved 79 police and 22 immigration officers. Although the information on which the raid was mounted referred to West African workers, all the non-European workers on the premises including those of Asian origin, a total of 47, were questioned: 31 people were arrested, 20 of whom were charged with immigration offences.

Following this series of raids, the Home Office made it known that since the beginning of 1980 there had been six joint service raids. On each occasion more than 20 people had been questioned about their immigration status. In addition to those just described, these raids had taken place at 'various premises' in the Blackburn area on 22 January, 'various premises' in the London area on 2 February, and at the Shell Centre in London on 29 March.[29]

The raids of May and June 1980 brought a considerable wave of protest, unparalleled since the Immigration Act had been in force. On 7 June, Brent Indian Association and Brent Trades Council, along with other bodies, mounted a picket of the main police station in Kilburn, the operations centre for the Bestways raid. And following the Main Gas raid a joint statement was issued by the general secretaries of the Transport and General Workers Union and the General and Municipal Workers Union. They said that such raids were producing a situation which was 'more reminiscent of the apartheid situation in South Africa than in Britain. We condemn repression of this sort in South Africa and the Soviet Union. We must condemn it here too.'[30]

Contrary to the evidence of those who had been held and questioned, Home Office minister Timothy Raison maintained in parliament that 'no blanket raids have been carried out'. He also stated that that 'there is no need for anybody to carry a passport with him [sic]. The only people who need worry about our immigration laws are those who are in breach of them.'[31] However, responding to the hostility to which the raids had given rise, Home Secretary William Whitelaw announced, only a few weeks after Raison's statement to parliament, that there would be a review of the procedures followed in joint operations by police and immigration officers. This review, Whitelaw hoped, 'will enable us to find ways of enforcing the law without damage to good race relations in this country'.[32]

The outcome of the review was made known to parliament and the public in December 1980, although the Metropolitan Police had issued force instructions setting out the new procedure some three months earlier. When Liberal peer Lord Avebury questioned this discrepancy he was told by the government that the timing of publication of orders to the Metropolitan Police was a matter for the Metropolitan Police Commissioner.[33] The Home Secretary said that after discussions with the Metropolitan Police and the Association of Chief Police Officers (which represents all the chief constables in the country) it had been agreed that every effort should be made before an operation took place to identify those people who were suspected of committing an immigration offence. In addition, the local police community liaison officer was to be consulted in all cases. Where people were questioned and eliminated from suspicion they should be subject to no further inconvenience, and if innocence could be established within a short time, for example by calling at a nearby address, then this course of action should always be considered. When people were taken to police stations, all enquiries were to be conducted as a matter of urgency so as to minimise any period of detention.[34]

The review of procedures and the announcement of its outcome were an exercise in public relations by a government embarrassed at the effect of the early 1980 raids. It restated that the police and the immigration service had a right to carry out raids and to demand to see passports. It also confirmed that it was in effect for those suspected of a breach of immigration law to prove their innocence, rather than for the police or immigration service to establish guilt.

Nothing was said which would not be expected as a matter of course in other police investigations. For example, it should be normal procedure that someone eliminated from suspicion would be subjected to no further inconvenience and that the period of detention should be kept to a minimum. Many people pointed out that there had been successive passport raids followed by successive official assurances which had done little either to change procedures and operations, or to alleviate the fears of those subject to questioning and detention. Such scepticism was soon confirmed.

In February 1981, two months after the review was announced, 12 Bengali restaurant workers in north London were woken by police and immigration officers and told to produce their passports. No arrests were made. Camden Committee for Community Relations commented that the raid had contravened a number of the points made in the Home Office review. Neither the local police commander nor the local community liaison officer had been informed of the operation beforehand, and the requirement that every effort be made to identify a suspect beforehand to avoid the harassment of innocent people did not appear to have been followed.[35] Home Office minister Timothy Raison attempted to defend the raid on the ground that it was not a 'major operation', which was the subject of the review, but a 'routine one', in which case 'some of the points covered by the review . . . could not realistically be applied'.[36]

The month after the north London raid, another major raid took place at the Sol Cafe factory in Greenford, Middlesex. At 5.15 a.m., just before the night shift was due to finish, about 50 police and immigration officers sealed off all exits from the premises, took over the gatehouse and placed an officer on each of the phones. The night management directed the officers to named individuals who were then taken off for questioning. One was subsequently released after satisfying the officers that his presence in the country was lawful. Four others were held as overstayers or illegal entrants.[37]

In January 1982 a raid on Smith's Meters in south west London 'netted' nine people in breach of immigration law, and a raid on the Shell Mex House in the Strand, central London, in April, in which 20 people were questioned, led to the identification of seven people as illegal entrants or overstayers.

The Sol Cafe raid is typical of the raids which have been mounted since the 1980 review. Since then, the available evidence suggests that the police have known whom they wanted to interview at specific places and have not engaged in 'fishing expeditions' such as the raid on Bestways. This is not to say that innocent people have *not* been questioned, detained or otherwise inconvenienced. They have, but not in such numbers as occurred before the 1980 review. The protests which have followed each passport raid, and in particular, the protests which followed the 1980 raids, therefore achieved some success in halting police excesses. What they did not, and could not, do was stop the raids altogether; as the 1980 review affirmed, under the existing system of immigration control such operations are basically lawful. Whether, however, they have a right to carry out such operations in the precise way in which they have done is another matter altogether and one which has not been resolved.

Under paragraph 17(1) of Schedule 2 of the Immigration Act 1971 a person liable to be detained, for example because s/he is an illegal entrant or has been refused leave to enter on arrival, may be arrested without a warrant by a police or immigration officer. This does not give police or immigration officers the right to enter premises to look for someone who is liable to be detained. Paragraph 17(2) enables the police (although not immigration officers) to apply to a magistrate for a warrant to enter and search premises. The paragraph makes it clear that the premises must be named in the warrant. What is not clear is whether the person whom the police wish to arrest must also be named in the warrant, and it is this question which has caused considerable controversy, particularly over the 1980 raids when the warrants clearly did not name particular individuals, but were used to detain and question a number of people apparently at random.

The paragraph in question states that police can obtain a warrant 'to enter, if need be by force, the premises named in the warrant for the purpose of searching for and arresting that person'. The apparent meaning of this paragraph – that the warrant name a specific person – was for a time accepted by the Home Office. In 1979, Home Office minister Brynmor John said in a letter to the Joint Council for the Welfare of Immigrants that it was the Home Office view that 'a search warrant obtained under the Immigration Act 1971 would restrict the police to searching for a specific named person'.[38] Following the 1980 raids, however, where the warrants did not name specific people, John claimed that the Act was now being interpreted differently under the Conservative government. He said that when he was in office specific advice was given by the Metropolitan Police that warrants could only be applied for where specific individuals were named. The Home Office, however, said that it had received legal advice that there was nothing in the Immigration Act to suggest that a specific person had to be named in the warrant. Whatever the legally correct interpretation of the paragraph, the fact remained that the law was being used in a different way and that there had been a change in the Home Office view. As JCWI's general secretary, Ian Martin commented at the time. 'The fact is that at one time the police's understanding of the law was otherwise, and this was presumably not just off the top of their heads.'[39]

There is however a strong legal argument that the paragraph requires the naming of specific individuals, as Ian MacDonald has pointed out. Firstly, the paragraph refers to 'a person liable to be arrested' and states that the warrant is to enable the arrest of 'that person'. Unless magistrates are given the name of the person or other clear means of identification it is difficult to see how they can be satisfied that there is someone liable to be arrested, and the paragraph makes it clear that the warrant only authorises the search for and arrest of that person. Secondly, the naming and identifying of specific people makes the task of the police much clearer when they arrive on premises and avoids the accusation that they are simply using the warrant as an excuse to carry out a fishing expedition in the hope that they may land some people who may be in breach of immigration law. Thirdly, the warrant is more akin to an arrest warrant than a search warrant since its primary purpose is not to search but to enable an arrest to be made. Arrest warrants granted under the Magistrates Court Act 1980 must always name or otherwise identify the persons to whom the warrants relate. Finally, if the intention of parliament is that a person need not be named in a warrant it is the normal practice for this to be stated explicitly. For example, the Mental Health Act 1959 specifically states that in the case of a warrant authorising the police to enter premises and remove someone who is suffering from mental disorder, 'it shall not be necessary . . . to name the person concerned'. In other words, although the matter is far from conclusive, there are strong grounds for the argument that warrants authorising the entry of premises under the Immigration Act should name those people liable to be detained.[40]

### Individual harassment

In April 1980, Home Office minister Timothy Raison told Alex Lyon MP that black people were not obliged to produce their passports, adding that there was no provision empowering anyone to require the production of a passport of someone who had been allowed into the UK.[41] Despite such an official position, there have been a considerable number of reported cases where black people have been asked by the police to produce their passports to establish the legality of their presence in the UK. In 1978, the JCWI bulletin, *Immigrant Voice*, reported the following cases: a Nigerian who was arrested when he contacted the police to volunteer bail for a friend who had been arrested on a minor criminal charge; a Ghanaian who was staying with a friend and arrested after police called looking for someone else; a Spaniard arrested when he went to a police station to ask for directions; a Ghanaian who reported the burglary of his home to the police whose investigation turned into an inquiry about his immigration status and that of his wife, and led to their arrest; an Egyptian arrested for no apparent reason while sightseeing in central London.[42]

The following year, the Scottish Council for Civil Liberties complained to the Scottish Office about the practice of demanding passports and, in particular, an incident where the Asian owner of licensed premises had been asked for his passport after selling alcohol to people believed to be under age. The Scottish Office responded that guidance to chief constables about the procedures to be followed when making enquiries into illegal immigrants had been issued in August 1973 and that this was in general observed by the police. In this particular case, however, the police officers had been acting in accordance with force orders which had not been amended to take this into account. The force, Lothian and Borders Police, expressed regret that the man had been asked to produce his passport and were said to be revising urgently their force instructions.[43]

At the same time this problem was highlighted in England by the evidence given to the Royal Commission on Criminal Procedure by the Joint Council for the Welfare of Immigrants and the Institute of Race Relations. JCWI's evidence included the following cases: a man who noticed an unusual number of police officers near his home and, on asking what had happened was asked whether he had any right to be in the country and was taken home by the police to produce his passport; a man who was stopped by police accused of theft from a shop and who, on convincing the police he was not the man they wanted, was then questioned about his immigration status; a man who took his car for its MOT test and was questioned by police not only about the car but also about his immigration status. Similar cases cited by the Institute of Race Relations included that of a black youth stopped on his way to school and detained for one and a half hours because he could not produce his passport; and the case of an Asian anti-racist demonstrator who was assaulted by a National Front supporter only to be arrested and detained on suspicion of being an illegal entrant.[44]

The Royal Commission eventually decided not to consider police powers under immigration law, even though both the JCWI and the Institute of Race Relations had established that police methods and practices were doing considerable harm to relations between the police and black people. Discussion of the issue was therefore excluded from the Commission's report. The practice meanwhile continued.

In 1981, a Southampton bus driver who was involved in a minor traffic incident was required to produce his passport by the police.[45] In 1982, an Asian family claimed that police refused to investigate a £15,000 burglary until they had produced their passports.[46] In January 1983, three Nigerian students who called the police to hand over a white intruder they had caught, were held in custody for 14 hours until they had established the legality of their presence in the UK. The alleged intruder was meanwhile allowed to go free.[47]

The police have the right to question anyone they wish in the investigation of a criminal offence, although generally no one is under any obligation to answer and no one can be arrested for obstruction of the police if they refuse to do so. Only immigration officers – and not the police – have the right to require the production of a passport; this power is limited to ports of entry. Unlike driving licences, which must be produced if required by the police, passports cannot be demanded from anyone outside disembarkation points.

The police do, of course, have the power to arrest someone for a breach of immigration law, but they must have 'reasonable cause' for suspecting that the person has committed such an offence. There is no clear definition of what this means although it does require, not only that the police officer genuinely believes that s/he had reasonable cause, but also that the cause must *in fact* be demonstrably reasonable. One of the problems is that the powers of arrest under the Immigration Act have not been tested in court. But it does seem clear that it is not lawful to arrest someone simply because he or she cannot produce a passport, far less to arrest someone because he or she is black.

## Marriage snooping

Arguments about police powers are not academic because the role of the police in the enforcement of the immigration laws has increased. During the period covered in this chapter, police involvement has increased in two important ways. First, as a result of changes made to the Immigration Rules in 1977, affecting the right to entry of foreign fiancés and husbands, the police became more involved in the investigation of marriages to see whether they were 'marriages of convenience'. Second, in 1979, the police took on the duty of serving notices on people refused extensions of their stay in Britain.

As we saw, the Labour government in 1977 responded to allegations that 'marriages of convenience' were being used to get round the immigration laws by changing the Immigration Rules, requiring foreign husbands to go through a 'probationary period' before they were allowed to settle in the UK. This was not only discriminatory on the grounds of sex in that it refused women the automatic right to be joined by foreign husbands and fiancés, while giving this right to men. It also opened the way to the surveillance and investigation of the private lives of many people where the Home Secretary had to be satisfied that the marriage was not 'one of convenience entered into primarily to obtain settlement here with no intention that the parties should live together permanently as man and wife'.[48]

In order to satisfy the immigration authorities that these conditions were met, couples were subjected to visits by the immigration authorities and the police, who conducted interrogations of a highly personal nature. One Pakistani man, in a typical interview, was asked a series of questions including: the names of everyone in the house, where each of these people slept, whether he had decorated his bedroom himself, what this decoration was like, for how long he and his wife had practised contraception, and when they had stopped doing so. An Indian man, married to a British citizen of Asian origin, was asked whether his marriage was an arranged marriage or a 'love marriage'; where he had spent his honeymoon; whether he and his wife had slept in the dining room; and whether he and his wife normally slept together. (When the man asked what was meant in this case by 'normally', the interviewer said, 'normally'. The man responded, 'Do you sleep with your wife normally or always?', whereupon the interviewer blushed and passed on to the next question.)

In these cases, questioning has been carried out by immigration officials, but in other cases the police have also been involved. A Pakistani couple who were interviewed at the Home Office were subsequently visited by three people, including a uniformed police officer. The couple had not been informed of their visit in advance. The husband was at work, but his wife, who was at home, was questioned in detail and the house was searched thoroughly, especially the couple's bedroom where all items of male clothing were carefully examined, as was personal correspondence. After about an hour, the three people left saying that they would come back. They returned about one week later, again when the husband was at work. Again the house was searched thoroughly and again the woman was questioned. A third visit was made about six weeks later. In another case, where the couple had not even yet been interviewed by the Home Office, police officers called to interview them at their home.[49]

An editorial in *Police Review*, objecting to the increasing role of the police in the enforcement of the immigration laws, noted that during one week in one 'modest Metropolitan station' there were no fewer than 19 files awaiting completion, each containing a list of questions specifically drafted by the Home Office. These questions, the editorial said, included:

> such gems as, 'Did you see any photographs indicating that the subject's marriage was a stable one?', 'Do the wife's parents approve of the marriage?', and 'Do you believe your "au pair" to be sexually promiscuous?'[50]

Such investigation of marriages continues under the present rules and, according to the Joint Council for the Welfare of Immigrants:

> immigration officials are continuing to pry into the personal
> lives of individuals in an offensive and wholly unjustified way
> . . . couples who fear that anger or refusal to discuss personal
> matters may prejudice the husband's chances of remaining
> here are unlikely to complain.[51]

The involvement of the police in marriage cases also brought
to light a longstanding arrangement between the Home Office
and registrars of marriages whereby the Home Office was
informed of suspected 'marriages of convenience'. The Joint
Council for the Welfare of Immigrants took up the case of a
Moroccan woman who was arrested in 1978 at Paddington register office after the registrar had seen her passport and had
contacted the Home Office. Enquiries revealed that it had been
standard practice since as long ago as 1925 for the Home Office
to be notified where local registrars have 'good reason' to believe
that a proposed marriage has been arranged for the 'sole purpose
of evading immigration controls'. Home Office minister Shirley
Sumerskill told JCWI that the arrangement was 'valuable' and she
would not ask the Registrar General to bring it to an end. The
Registrar General also said that local registrars were instructed
to inform his office where they had good reason to believe that
the marriage was being contracted for the purpose of evading
immigration control or acquiring British citizenship. They were
not, however, required to notify the Registrar General where a
party to a marriage had overstayed their leave to be in the UK.
This was left to the discretion of the registrar 'as the man on the
spot'. If such a case was reported to the Registrar General the
Home Office would be notified if it appeared to be 'sound'.

Register offices therefore act as agents of immigration control
by notifying the Home Office about cases believed to involve
so-called 'marriages of convenience' and overstayers. In carrying
out this role, registrars can ask to see the passports of people who
are seeking to get married; although this is justified by the
Registrar General on the grounds that registrars must ensure
that accurate information is recorded in the official marriage
registers and that it is necessary to know the nationality of the
parties to a marriage. In practice, however, it appears that only
black people are required to produce their passports. In 1983, for

example, MP Denis Howell said that he had recently attended the wedding of a black constituent who had been required by the register office to produce his passport. And in the same year, the London Borough of Camden apologised to a black woman who had been asked for her passport when she applied for a marriage certificate. The woman was a naturalised British citizen who had lived in the UK for 12 years. Her offer to the registrar of a birth certificate to provide proof of identity, date of birth and so on, had been refused.[52]

## Deportation: detection and surveillance

Notices of refusal for people refused extensions of their stay in the UK had formerly been sent by registered letter. The Association of Chief Police Officers, representing all chief constables and assistant chief constables, argued that this should be a police function and in 1979 the Home Office sent a circular to all police forces explaining the new police role.[53] Initially, the refusal notices would be served only on those who applied for an extension after their original leave had expired, but that in future the police would be required to serve refusal notices on others too.

The chief constables may have been keen for greater police involvement in the enforcement of immigration control, but other ranks took a different view. The ACPO suggestion was roundly condemned by the police magazine, *Police Review*, which described it as 'incredible'. Everyone, the journal's editorial suggested, should ask themselves the question: 'Should the supervision of immigrants be a part of the Police function?'. The magazine clearly thought that it should not, and complained that 'the overworked officers who are in charge of our undermanned police stations have another cross to carry'.[54]

Similar criticism was made by the general secretary of JCWI, Ian Martin, who said that the new arrangement would not only be inefficient but would waste considerable police resources. In addition, it would result in an increasing number of expensive prosecutions of people who would otherwise have left voluntarily and would give rise to unwarranted police questioning of the status of other immigrants at the addresses at which the refusal notice had to be served. It would therefore further damage relations between the police and the public.[55]

Such objections were not, however, accepted by the Home Office. The Minister of State, Lord Harris, replied that the police were not an inappropriate body to be involved in the enforcement of immigration control since certain evasions of immigration control, including overstaying, were criminal offences. Police officers serving refusal notices, he said, would go to addresses with a specific task related to the person named in the notice and there was therefore no reason why anyone lawfully present in the UK should have anything to fear. Such visits should not therefore cause damage to relations between the police and the immigrant community.[56]

The police were given this new function in addition to the powers they already had to detect and apprehend overstayers, who are liable to immediate arrest. Many of those who are arrested come to the attention of the police during the kind of random questioning and demands for passports described earlier. In addition, police enquiries may be initiated by the special overstayers tracing units of the Home Office who inform the police if they believe that someone has not left the country when they should have done.

Although overstaying is a criminal offence, it can arise for a number of reasons and may, in any case, only be a matter of staying beyond one's permitted time by a few days or weeks. People may overstay by mistake or misunderstanding, they may lose their passports, they or a relative may be ill, and so on. Take for example a case reported by the Joint Council for the Welfare of Immigrants.

Cetin was a Turkish seaman who came to the UK on the advice of his doctor to recuperate from an illness. His leave to remain expired the day before New Year's Eve and he planned to travel to Italy on New Year's Day to start a new job which he had been promised. He did not think that it was necessary to renew his leave as he thought that the Home Office would be closed. In any case, he thought, it was only a matter of staying an extra two days. After a disturbance at a party in a home where Cetin was staying, the police were called and discovered that Cetin's leave to remain had expired. Even though he had all his luggage with him ready to depart and a voucher for an air ticket to Italy, Cetin was arrested. He was held in custody for nine days, taken to court, convicted, recommended for deportation, and held in Ashford Remand Centre for three months before being deported.[57]

The police are also involved in the enforcement of internal immigration controls through reporting to the Home Office offences committed by people who are liable to deportation, that is people who are not British citizens or who were not patrial when the British Nationality Act came into force in January 1983. This practice became clear in August 1980 when the *Guardian* reported the case of a man, born in Singapore but resident in the UK for 20 years, who had pleaded guilty to a driving offence and been fined £20. Two weeks later, an officer from the local police force in Hampshire telephoned him at his place of work asking him for various personal details including his country of origin and the number of his passport. The man questioned the relevance of this information but arranged that the police officer call at his home. There the questions were repeated and the officer showed the man a form headed, 'Report for the information of the Under Secretary of State, Home Office on the conviction of an alien/Commonwealth citizen'. The form included sections, 'Recommended for deportation' and 'Special Branch informed'.[58]

The matter was taken up with Home Office minister, Timothy Raison, who strongly denied that there was any kind of register of convictions of aliens or others liable to deportation. He did, however, admit in a letter to Lord Avebury that:

> courts were long ago asked to notify to the Home Office cases in which a recommendation for deportation had been made, and the police to report on the facts. Additionally . . . the police were asked to notify to the Home Office details of cases in which foreign nationals were convicted of offences which might properly be regarded as serious enough to merit deportation but where no recommendation had been made by the court.

The minister went on to say that there was no real inconsistency between this practice which was essential to the 'proper exercise of immigration control' and the advice given to the police in 1973 that they should avoid taking measures which might be construed as harassment of immigrants. The minister would accept only that the case had illustrated that the guidance given to the police by the Home Office was inadequate since:

It is far from the intention of the Home Office that the police should report all offences by non-patrial members of the community to the Immigration and Nationality Department, or that oppressive procedures should be employed to establish the immigration status of people questioned by the police in connection with the investigation of crime.

The revised guidelines issued to the police state that reports should continue to be submitted in respect of people who are convicted and who are liable to deportation. A report should be made in any case of conviction punishable with imprisonment (in practice this means the vast majority of offences) where the person has been in the UK for less than five years or is still subject to a time limit. Where a person has been in the UK for five years, a report should be made where an immediate or suspended custodial sentence has been imposed.

Even though convicted people may not be deported as a result of police reports, the information will nevertheless go on file and will be available to be considered when, for example, they apply to have conditions attached to their stay removed, or apply for British nationality.

The Royal Commission on Criminal Procedure which was set up in 1977 to review police powers and the criminal process provided an important opportunity to review police enforcement of the immigration laws. In 1979, the Commission, which had invited submissions from a wide range of bodies and individuals, received two important documents which dealt with police involvement in the immigration laws. The Institute of Race Relations, looking at the issue in the context of relations between the police and black people generally, argued forcefully for the repeal of the powers of arrest and detention given to the police and immigration officers and the repeal too of the Immigration Act's penal provisions. The Institute said that these:

make every black person in this country a potential suspect in the eyes of the police, and the harassment and suffering they create for many people is not justified by the number of 'real' illegal immigrants detained. Also we believe that these provisions help create an attitude towards black people which is incompatible with the police's function of protecting all sections of the community.[59]

Similarly the Joint Council for the Welfare of Immigrants argued that 'a major cause of the suspicion and mistrust with which the police were viewed by many within the immigrant community' was the role of the police in the enforcement of immigration control. In addition, JCWI argued, the very existence of criminal penalties for breaches of immigration law and the wide powers of arrest available to the police, which defined immigration offences as a serious threat to society, contributed to a hardening of attitudes towards immigrants on the part of society as a whole, and the police in particular.[60]

Such arguments were ignored by the Royal Commission which decided that the immigration laws did not fall within its remit, even though the enforcement of these laws, as the Institute of Race Relations and the Joint Council for the Welfare of Immigrants clearly showed, had major implications for police/black relations generally.

## Workplace controls

One important effect of the passport raids, particularly those of 1980, was that more employers carry out their own passport checks so as to avoid raids by the police and the immigration service. Within one week of the Bestways raid, for example, a laundry in Chingford, Essex, which employed a large number of Asian workers, had told all their black workers to bring their passports to work and establish their right to be in the UK. The personnel officer said that it was standard practice to ask for the passports or birth certificates of non-white [sic] workers, and added, 'I do know that there are other firms that do go into it as we do.'[61] Similarly, the management of the Hilton Hotel in London admitted that since the raids they had become 'ever more vigilant in making sure that we do not employ illegal immigrants by checking on their passports and any correspondence they may have had with the Home Office'.[62]

The practice of checking passports had already been endorsed by the authorities. For example an industrial tribunal ruled in 1978 that the Post Office had not unlawfully discriminated on racial grounds by asking a black applicant for a sorter's job to produce his passport before he was further considered.[63] Such a ruling, coupled with the fact that the passport checking was being done by a major public body, must have served as proof that there was nothing objectionable in the practice.

Some years later, the No Pass Laws Here Group, which had been formed to monitor internal controls, found from a small survey of London local authorities that several admitted to checking the passports of people who applied for work. The London Borough of Lewisham, for example, said that successful applicants for jobs were required to produce their passports, although it maintained that this was required of *all* applicants regardless of their colour. Similarly, the London Borough of Wandsworth stated that any applicants who said that they were subject to conditions relating to taking employment were asked to produce their passports. The Council claimed that this was applied to all applicants regardless of their colour. The London Borough of Tower Hamlets also admitted that if it appeared likely that an applicant would need a work permit he or she might be asked to produce a passport.[64]

In the London Borough of Camden, however, the practice of passports checking had been stopped in 1981 after representations from the local council for community relations. Following a case where a black applicant for a council post had been told by the director of the department concerned that he would 'require sight of your passport', new instructions were issued within the Council that although applicants for jobs were to be asked whether they were subject to any restrictions on taking employment, if the answer to this question was 'yes', then no documentary evidence should be required. In no circumstances, the instructions said, should a departmental staffing officer ask a job applicant to produce a passport. Where there was good reason to suspect that information was being deliberately concealed – and the grounds for suspicion had to be 'other than racial' – the matter had to be referred to a higher authority for consideration of any action to be taken.

A similar instruction to stop the passport checking of job applicants was issued by the Inner London Education Authority in 1981. However, ILEA substituted a requirement that applicants must sign a statement indicating that they were not restricted in taking employment; that the Authority reserved the right to seek from the applicant verification of the factual basis of any information provided; and that the applicant accepted that the discovery of any legal impediment after an appointment had been made would lead to immediate dismissal.

ILEA's justification for requiring applicants to sign this intimidating statement was that they had a legal duty to establish proof of eligibility to work in the country. As we have seen, other employers have also given this as their reason for requiring to see the passports of job applicants. In fact, there is no obligation on employers to check the immigration status of employees or to check that job applicants are authorised to work in this country. While the Immigration Act of 1971 makes it an offence for someone to break any condition attached to their stay and it is therefore also an offence for someone who is not authorised to work to take up employment, it is not an offence for an employer to engage someone who is not supposed to work. At least one government minister has tried to get round this by claiming that it is an offence under the Magistrates Court Act 1980 for someone to aid and abet a person to break the law. Lord Gowrie said:

> Employers do therefore need to know what they are about and it would not be unreasonable for them to ask employees and job applicants to produce passports etc, where they have good reason to suspect that employment restrictions are being deliberately concealed, provided of course that such enquiries do not discriminate between racial groups.[65]

It was precisely on this interpretation of the Magistrates Court Act that ILEA based its requirement, even though Lord Gowrie's reference had been described by the senior legal officer of the Commission for Racial Equality as 'misconceived'. In a letter to ILEA, the Commission had said that all that the Act did was to extend the offence of aiding, abetting, counselling or procuring to summary offences, only insofar as these were not covered by existing legislation. It did not change the nature of the offence and did not place any positive duty on employers to ensure that the commission of an offence was not being aided. An employer would only be liable if the prosecution could prove that s/he had either desired the offence to be committed or was 'recklessly indifferent' as to whether it was committed or not.

In other words, there is no legal requirement that employers check the passports of their employees and job applicants. It is therefore not only unnecessary, but also presumably contrary to the race relations legislation, in that it almost invariably applies only to black people and not to whites. Despite this, Lord Gowrie's statement was an encouragement and official sanction of the practice of passport checking by employers.

## Conclusion

The period reviewed in this chapter was of crucial importance in the development of internal controls. The Home Office continued its wide interpretation of the law and in this received the full support of the courts, at least until it was realised that they might have gone too far. The fact that the House of Lords did something of an about-turn in 1983 in the case of *Khawaja* when it held that immigrants did not owe any positive 'duty of candour' should not lead us to forget the process which had gone before. The Lords' decision was not the result of some liberal high-mindedness or generosity. It is reasonable to assume that the Lords were moved to act, not just by the almost unprecedented criticism which followed the 1980 *Zamir* decision, but by developments in society at large and, in particular, the urban riots of 1981. It would be absurd to suggest that people rioted because of *Zamir*, or even because of immigration law generally. But it would be equally absurd to deny that there was *any* connection, that those who took to the streets in the summer of 1981 were completely unaware of and unconcerned about the effect of immigration controls, both as passed by parliament and as interpreted by the Home Office and the courts, on the black communities. The House of Lords must have been acutely aware of the feelings in those communities. It cannot have been complete coincidence that one of the judges hearing the 1983 case was also the man who had conducted the official investigation in the Brixton riots, Lord Scarman.

In any case, despite the 1983 ruling, the role of the courts in immigration cases under the 1971 Act remains a shameful episode in British judicial history. Civil liberties were thrown to the winds as the judges confirmed the racism of immigration controls and so simply subjected more and more people to the mercy of the authorities.

In the context of this judicially-approved racism, the police considerably extended their involvement in the enforcement of the immigration laws, both by increasing their activities in passport raids and checks, and in their new-found roles investigating marriages and serving refusal notices.

Together, the Home Office, the courts and the police brought the number of people removed as alleged illegal entrants and those deported, to their highest ever levels. In 1978, 540 people were removed as alleged illegal entrants while 1,234 deportation orders were made. In 1980, the numbers had risen to 910 removals and 2,472 deportation orders. In the five years from 1978 to 1982, some 3,320 people were removed and 9,162 deportation orders made.[66]

The enforcement of the immigration laws spread into other areas, particularly employment, where employers increasingly took it upon themselves, with the encouragement of the government, to carry out their own checks on immigration status. Most insidiously, internal controls spread during this period into the provision of public services and benefits and it is this area that the next chapter examines.

# 4. Second-class claimants

The shift in the ideology of immigration control around 1977/78 described in the last chapter did not just result in harsher policing of the immigration laws. It also led to one of the most important developments in internal controls, that of the increased connection between immigration and the welfare state.

For Commonwealth citizens the connection dates largely from the Immigration Act of 1971. Since the Act came into force an increasing number of people have been allowed entry into Britain only on condition that they do not have 'recourse to public funds'. Such people now include students, visitors and their dependants, fiancés (until the time of their marriage), fiancées, and the dependants of people who were not settled here when the Immigration Act came into force. As we also saw, there have been reported instances of black people being required to produce their passports before being granted services or benefits.

There have been a number of novel features in the post-1977 developments. First, there was a climate of panic about immigration, where the terms of the 'debate' shifted rapidly from the question of people coming in to the country to those already here. The security of black people settled here became threatened by the wave of violence and harassment which followed the talk of illegal immigration, marriages of convenience and overstaying. Black people were suspected, either of having overstayed, or of trying to claim a benefit or service to which they were not entitled.

Second, the connections between immigration and the welfare state which developed after 1977 were the result of government policy and legislation. Previously it could be argued that passport checking had been carried out on a basis which was largely individual, dependent on the whim of this or that official. Government spokespeople would claim, of course, that they had not intended to implement forms of internal control. But even if this were true, black people and others had warned of the consequences of their policies and actions: internal control would be the logical and foreseeable result of the changes being made.

This chapter looks at the main areas of state services and benefits – education, health, housing and social security. In each case it shows the connections between such services and immigration status. Immigration status has come to affect access to services or benefits, and vice versa; consequently there has been a growing liaison between those administering the benefit or service and the immigration authorities. The law in this respect is often complex, but it has been made even more complex by the persistent refusal of the government to provide a definition of 'recourse to public funds'.

## Education

Government action has led to increased internal controls and surveillance, particularly in relation to those attending higher education institutions, but also for those attending school. As we saw in Chapter 2, black children in Ealing in 1974 had been required to produce their passports before being admitted to school (see page 33) and in 1978 it was reported that a British-born black girl had been told by her local education authority to produce her passport before she would be admitted, even though she had produced her birth certificate which showed that she had been born in Bristol.[1] In 1980, Alex Lyon MP raised with the government a circular which the Director of Education in Sheffield had sent to all schools instructing them to ask for passports where a child was in the country without his or her parents or where the length of the child's stay was in doubt. Home Office minister Timothy Raison denied that the circular might be unlawful since schools had no obligation to admit children who were here without their parents or who were only here for a few months. In an important statement Raison gave further official support for the practice of passport checking:

As far as we are aware there is no provision empowering anyone to require a person after he has been allowed to enter the United Kingdom to produce his passport, apart from the powers given to police registration officers in respect of aliens required to register with the police. There are, however, many circumstances in which the production of a passport is the most simple way of establishing identity, status or eligibility for some benefit, and it would seem a pity not to be able to suggest to those of us who possess passports the usefulness of the facility they afford.[2]

Given this reply, passport checking by education authorities and schools has continued and in 1981 an Asian woman taking her two children to a school in Newham, east London, to register them for their first term was told by the school that she should go home and bring the children's passports.[3]

Although schools are not obliged to enrol pupils who are only temporarily in the country, in 1981 the courts laid down in the case of *Ved* that immigration status is not affected by seeking state education. Before then, the Home Office had argued that state education amounted to 'recourse to public funds'. In other words, people admitted to this country on condition that they did not have recourse to public funds were expected to provide private education for their children. The Ved family had been admitted as people of independent means for a limited period. Extensions had been granted from time to time, but in 1979 the Home Office refused an application for a further extension. The family therefore appealed to an immigration adjudicator. He too rejected their case. If the family were to be treated as people of independent means, he said, their means had to be assessed on the basis that the children attended fee paying schools, since for them to attend state schools would amount to recourse to public funds. The Court of Appeal rejected this argument, saying that a distinction had to be made between matters such as supplementary benefit, employment benefit and pensions which were recourse to public funds, and facilities provided by the state, such as education, which were not.[4]

Although the ruling applies to students in further and higher education, this does not mean that all students are treated alike. Since 1967, a distinction has been made for fee purposes between 'home' students and those from overseas, the latter having to pay higher fees than the former. Ten years later, the Department of Education and Science took steps which were to increase internal controls and surveillance of black students. Advice was sent to local education authorities and educational institutions defining 'overseas' students as those who had not been 'ordinarily resident' or resident in the UK for three years before commencing their course. In 1978 the DES stated that 'ordinary residence' had to be interpreted according to the place of a person's 'real home'. The immediate reasons for this advice were twofold. The Race Relations Act 1976 threatened to make the differential fees policy unlawful as being indirect discrimination. The DES advice assured education authorities, universities and colleges that the policy would be covered by the exemptions provided for in the new law and they would not therefore be discriminatory. Some education authorities had been complaining that overseas students were achieving 'home' status by spending three years at private schools or further education institutions. The DES advice encouraged education authorities to investigate whether the UK had been a student's 'real home'.

The differential fees policy and the DES advice which accompanied it operated as internal immigration controls in two ways. For many education authorities the simplest way of ascertaining whether someone was an 'overseas' student has been to demand to see the passport of anyone who is black. As a result of the 1978 DES advice, many local education authorities decided that people who were admitted to the UK as students did not become 'ordinarily resident' however long they studied here since they had come here for a special purpose – education – and the DES had indicated that those who came for such a special purpose might not be ordinarily resident. In addition, there was the issue of the 'real home' test suggested by the DES which led some authorities to decide that someone who was in the UK without their parents had not made the UK their 'real home'.

Such decisions were challenged by students who were refused grants. Nilish Shah, for example, had come to the UK from Kenya with his parents in 1976. Shortly after, his parents returned to Kenya where they remained. In 1979, Nilish Shah was refused a grant. Even though he had indefinite leave to remain in the UK, the London Borough of Barnet maintained that his 'real home' was in Kenya and that because he had been studying all the time he had been in the UK he had not been 'ordinarily resident' here. Abu Abdullah came to the UK from Bangladesh in 1975. He was given entry as a student and his visa was extended from time to time. In 1979 he was refused a grant for a degree course by Shropshire County Council which claimed that because he had only a limited leave to remain he could not be ordinarily resident.

These cases, along with four others, were heard by the Court of Appeal in 1981. It was decided in *Shah and others* that those who were in the UK without restriction were 'ordinarily resident', while those who had only limited leave were not.[5] Lord Denning, the presiding judge, thought the phrase 'ordinary residence' should not be given its ordinary meaning of 'habitually and normally resident . . . apart from temporary or occasional absences'. Instead it should be interpreted in the light of immigration law so as to exclude those who were not entitled to remain in the UK for ever.

The House of Lords rejected this approach in the following year.[6] It ruled that the words 'ordinarily resident' had no special or technical meaning for students; and simply meant living in a particular place 'voluntarily and for settled purposes as part of the regular order of one's life'. Such settled purposes would include education, and so a student could therefore be ordinarily resident.

The decision showed that the DES advice of 1978 had unwittingly led local education authorities to break the law. The government, however, moved quickly to reverse the law lords' judgement. Within months of the decision, new regulations were brought into force providing that even someone with three years' ordinary residence would be excluded from a mandatory grant if their residence had been 'wholly or mainly for the purposes of receiving full-time education', and that education authorities need not even consider giving discretionary awards to such people. Although a few students who had been wrongly classified as overseas students were able to claim retrospective awards following the House of Lords decision, those who gained most from the ruling were those who were in least need. Only those who had already proceeded with their proposed course of study despite being refused a grant could qualify for an award. Those who could not afford to continue when grants were withdrawn had no redress.[7]

Students are also subject to control through the liaison which exists between colleges and the Home Office. For example, when deciding whether to extend a student's stay the Home Office may request from his or her college information about the student's attendance at classes, examination record, educational ability and payment of fees. In one case Hull University even threatened to report its overseas students to the Home Office if they did not pay their fees promptly.[8]

Finally, although access to higher education is not considered to be recourse to public funds, this does not mean that students have a right to other benefits. The Home Office has made it clear, for example, that a student and any dependants in accommodation provided by a local authority under the Housing (Homeless Persons) Act 1977, or receiving a rent allowance or rate rebate, would be treated 'as having inadequate funds available and be refused an extension'.[9] The Home Office also says that it will only act if a case is brought to its attention and does not initiate its own enquiries.

It is clear that some local authorities routinely pass such information on to the Home Office. In Manchester, for example, the local authority admitted to passing information automatically, and in Aberdeen several students were advised that the Home Office would be informed if they did not stop receiving rent rebates.[10]

In several ways, therefore, education and immigration control have become closely connected. What developed in the area of education was to become a precedent for other areas.

## Health

As we saw in Chapter 2, the practice of passport checking in the health service was supposed to have been stopped following complaints in 1976 when 200 Asian women living in Leicester were required to produce their passports before being given ante-natal care. In 1979, however, apparently following allegations from NHS staff that the NHS was being abused by people not entitled to use it, the Department of Health and Social Security issued a circular which opened the way to even more checking. The circular, entitled 'Gatecrashers', was issued to all health authorities in the London area.[11] It advised medical and administrative staff that they had a part to play in ensuring eligibility for free treatment. Staff should watch out for visitors from abroad who were not 'ordinarily resident' in the UK and who were therefore not entitled to free treatment. The circular stressed that overseas visitors were eligible for free treatment only in emergencies if they came within the so-called 'Good Samaritan' policy – having fallen ill or had an accident in this country. Despite the allegations which had been made of abuse, however, the DHSS concluded that it was 'not aware of any evidence to support this inference'.[12] If this was the Department's conclusion, it is difficult to see the need for the circular in the first place. It seems more likely that the circular was the result, not just of pressure from staff about 'abuse' of the NHS, but also of a climate of opinion which encouraged hospital staff to look out for those who might be in breach of the immigration laws.

The 'Gatecrashers' circular increased the checking of the immigration status of patients by hospital staff and encouraged staff to refuse treatment to people whom they considered ineligible. In November 1979, for example, only one month after the circular had been issued, a Cypriot woman attended St Bartholomew's Hospital in London for an appointment with a consultant surgeon. A hospital clerk, suspicious of the woman's immigration status, contacted the DHSS which in turn checked with the Home Office, receiving an answer within minutes that the woman's appeal against deportation had been turned down. The clerk then informed the Department of the woman's home address and the date of her next appointment.

A formal complaint of breach of medical confidentiality was made to the British Medical Association by the surgeon, Martin Birstingl, although the health minister, Gerald Vaughan, stated that the patient's address and date of next appointment had neither been asked for, nor disclosed. The disclosure of information to other government departments about people seeking treatment was, he said, a matter of 'great delicacy' and such disclosure would be improper if it served the purposes of immigration control, unless it were done with the patient's express consent. The minister said that he had issued instructions that officials seeking information from the Home Office about a patient's eligibility for treatment should tell the Home Office nothing about the patient except the name and date of birth. [13]

The 'Gatecrashers' circular had, however, given encouragement to hospital officials to check the immigration status of patients and there were numerous cases of this in 1980. Leonis Peter Low, for example, was born at St Peter's Hospital in Paddington, London and was therefore a citizen of the UK and Colonies. The baby and her mother returned to Hong Kong where the child soon became seriously ill with a blood disease. Doctors advised that St Peter's was the only hospital which could provide the necessary treatment and so the mother returned to the UK with her baby. The hospital, however, refused to treat the child, saying that the decision had been made after consulting the DHSS, which had confirmed that there were no grounds on which to provide free treatment. [14]

In March 1980, the press reported that a Sri Lankan woman who had lived in Britain for eight years had been asked to produce her passport when she tried to make an appointment at an ante-natal clinic. The woman had been treated at the same hospital only months before without any problems and even though she provided details of her national insurance number, she was told by the booking clerk that she had also to provide her passport. Following the incident, the deputy house governor at St Stephen's Hospital in London said that requests for passports were made when the patient was suspected of being a foreign national who was not entitled to health service treatment. She said:

> It is just a matter of common sense, whether we go on their being foreign, or their colour or whatever. All we can do is ask someone politely if they can show their passport and if they do, then this immediately clarifies the matter. It is a practice that is well established, a lot of London hospitals do it. [15]

The government maintained that there had been no change in official policy since the statement by David Owen in 1976 and declined to condone the practice of requiring any particular group of people, *as a matter of routine*, to produce passports as a condition of obtaining treatment.

However, the government also attached 'great importance to the effective control by the National Health Service of visitors'. If staff found themselves in doubt about a patient's eligibility and were unable to resolve that doubt by further questioning, then 'they may properly ask for further documentary evidence, including passports . . . This must be done sensitively.'[16]

It was reported in June 1980 that British women who were working and living in Britain were being refused health service treatment on the ground that they were married to foreign men who were living abroad. They were not therefore considered to be 'ordinarily resident' in Britain and were as such excluded from free health service treatment.[17] In October the same year, Lulu Banu, a member of the Commission for Racial Equality, who had lived in the UK for 14 years, was asked to produce her passport before being admitted to St Stephen's Hospital, London. The hospital refused to accept as proof of eligibility either her own doctor's letter or the fact that she had been treated previously at the hospital.[18] In December, a visiting professor on a Commonwealth fellowship was also refused treatment at St Stephen's until he had produced his passport and a letter from his sponsoring body,[19] and in January 1981, the same hospital again refused treatment, on this occasion to a woman who was a refugee from Ethiopia.[20] At the same time a Pakistani doctor who practised in Nottingham told the *Guardian* that she had been refused ante-natal care when in London until she had produced her passport.

These cases illustrate how hospital staff, encouraged by the government, the DHSS and 'anti-scrounger' public opinion, took it on themselves to check the immigration status of patients and to act as agents of immigration control. They show too, how such checking, while justified as being aimed at those who were 'foreign' or visitors, inevitably included in its scope those who were neither foreign nor visitors, but simply not white.

The government announced in 1981 that virtually all visitors to the UK would be charged for use of the NHS. Social services minister Patrick Jenkin claimed that there was 'fairly widespread abuse by foreigners of the NHS', although he provided no evidence and this had been disputed by the DHSS 'Gatecrashers' circular. Hospitals, the minister said, could determine whether someone was eligible for free treatment by means of two or three simple questions 'supported by such evidence as might be necessary'. The change would supposedly save the NHS an estimated £5m each year.

The government's proposal was widely criticised. The Commission for Racial Equality, for example, said it was 'damaging to race relations and . . . inevitably discriminatory'. Similar criticisms were made by the Confederation of Health Service Employees and by the TUC itself. The JCWI pointed out that the proposal was being put forward at a time of increased passport checking by other authorities. If implemented, it would increase racial discrimination in the application of the eligibility tests to black people.

Under such pressure, the government modified the scheme but its essential features remained unchanged. It maintained that the principal of 'universal challenge' – that is questioning *everyone* about their eligibility – would prevent discrimination. Most of the organisations which opposed the scheme were extremely sceptical. It seemed most unlikely that hospital staff would question every patient; in practice challenges would be limited to those who appeared to them to be unlikely to be eligible for free treatment. As had happened under the old regulations, these would be mainly black people or others thought to be foreign. In other words, the new scheme would increase checks on immigration status and eligibility and lead to even greater harassment of black patients. It was also argued that the new charges scheme would lead to even more liaison between hospitals, the DHSS and the Home Office. The DHSS has always maintained that the confidentiality of the NHS would always be respected, although the 1979 case of the Cypriot woman quoted earlier shows that this is not as straightforward as it appears, nor have such ministerial assurances always been honoured in other contexts, as the other sections of this chapter show.

The new scheme for charging certain people from overseas came into effect in October 1982 with the support of the parliamentary Home Affairs Committee which had carried out an enquiry into the question and concluded that they would not be discriminatory. A minority report by the Labour members of the Committee dissented. John Wheeler MP, who chaired the Committee, stated that, 'So far as race relations are concerned, we consider they represent a positive step forward'.[21]

It is still too early to judge the practical effects of the scheme and the government's refusal to monitor the workings of the scheme and, in particular, to maintain a list of numbers and the home countries of those charged for treatment, does not help in analysing those effects. Some limited indication is, however, available.

One case cited by the Joint Council for the Welfare of Immigrants involved a woman who had lived in the UK since she was 14. Two years before the charges came into effect she married an Indian doctor and, because the immigration rules at the time prevented her from living with him here, she went to live with him in India. At the same time she applied for registration as a British citizen, a status to which she was entitled. The woman returned to England because she missed her friends and family and a few weeks later gave birth to a child in hospital. The delivery was difficult but this did not prevent hospital staff questioning the woman about her status three days after the birth. They decided that she was not ordinarily resident, even though she had lived in the UK since she was 14 and was still in the country nearly one year after the birth. She was sent a bill by the health authority for almost £800.[22] In another case reported in December 1982, an Indian visitor who had broken his leg was said to be liable to charges of £7,000 and that since he was unable to pay, the charge would fall on his sister and brother-in-law whom he had come to visit.[23] It was only following publicity about the case that the DHSS instructed the local health authority not to seek payment from relatives. It pointed out that although the woman in this case had signed an undertaking that she would pay the costs of treatment in the event of her brother's default, she need not have done so.[24] At the same time it was reported that Stoke Mandeville Hospital in Buckinghamshire was requiring those liable to charges to put down a deposit of £15,000 before they received treatment.[25]

The first six months of the charges scheme netted considerably less than the government had estimated. It was announced in

November 1983 that only £374,459 had been raised as compared with a promised £5m or £6m. Health minister Kenneth Clarke maintained that the six months in question were untypical since many health authorities had failed to start the scheme in time and there were fewer visitors than there would be in the latter half of the year. In addition some authorities apparently were not implementing the scheme at all and were failing to charge those who were ineligible for free treatment.[26]

Only a detailed investigation will show what the effect of the health charges scheme has been on black people living in this country. What seems clear, however, is that the government's proposals themselves fuelled and supported racism and xenophobia with their references to 'abuse' of the NHS.

## Housing

People who are neither British, nor EEC, nor Commonwealth citizens, who settled in the UK before 1973, (or their dependants), are required to show that they will have adequate accommodation before they are granted entry clearance. They can be refused entry if it is thought that they are likely to be homeless and so have recourse to public funds. Anyone admitted to the UK on condition that they do not have recourse to public funds is not supposed to seek housing under the provisions of the Housing (Homeless Persons) Act 1977. Doing so could well render them liable to deportation for breach of conditions. This does not apply where someone is incapable of maintaining him or herself and any family, or where circumstances have changed. But the Home Office could argue that it had been deceived about the accommodation which was said to exist and as a result could claim that the entry had been illegal.

Some local authorities have tried to evade their responsibilities for housing black people and people from abroad by claiming either that they have no 'local connection' or are 'intentionally homeless' and, as such, not entitled to housing as homeless persons. The first such case arose in 1978, the year of the Select Committee report and Margaret Thatcher's provocative comments about immigration. The London Borough of Hillingdon's housing committee, chaired by Terence Dicks (now a Tory MP), refused to authorise housing for a Kenyan widower and his family of four. The widower was a citizen of the UK and Colonies who had been forced to leave Kenya on the expiry of his work permit and had been admitted to Britain on a UK passport. The family were sent in a taxi to the Foreign Office which, Dicks claimed, was responsible for them. In contrast, the Council had found accommodation for a white family of nine who arrived three days earlier from what was then Rhodesia.[27] In the same year, Slough Council offered a homeless woman, married to an American serviceman, a loan to leave the country rather than meet its obligation to house her. The deputy leader of the Council stated candidly, 'For want of a better word this is a repatriation scheme . . . It's easier and cheaper to pay their fares than give them a house at the expense of Slough people'.[28]

The following year, Crawley Borough Council refused to house two Italian families who had been living with relatives since they came to the UK and had only sought public housing when they had eventually been asked to leave. Even though the families were EEC nationals and therefore supposedly entitled to the same rights as British workers, Lord Denning and the Court of Appeal agreed with the Council. Denning said:

> If any family from the Common Market can fly into Gatwick, stay a month or two with relatives and claim to be unintentionally homeless, it would be a most serious matter for the overcrowded borough. The borough should be able to do better than King Canute. He bade the rising tide at Southampton to come no further. It took no notice and he got his feet wet. I trust the councillors of Crawley will keep theirs dry against this new advancing tide.[29]

In 1980, however, the Court of Appeal rejected a similar argument from Hillingdon Borough Council which refused to house an Ethiopian refugee on the ground that she had no 'local connection'. In the lower court, Mr Justice Griffiths sympathised with the Council but said that strict immigration controls meant that 'all and sundry' did not arrive homeless from abroad. Similarly, in the Court of Appeal, Lord Denning said that the safeguard against abuse of the homelessness provision lay in the control exercised by the immigration authorities.[30]

The Court of Appeal returned to the question of the housing rights of immigrants in May 1981. The case concerned a Bangladeshi man, Taffazul Islam, who had lived in the UK since 1965 and was not therefore required to show immigration officers that he had adequate accommodation for his family when they wanted to join him. Yet, the Court of Appeal held that Islam had made himself and his family homeless intentionally by bringing them from Bangladesh without ensuring he had adequate accommodation for them. Lord Denning said that Islam's home was not in England, but in Bangladesh where the family lived and where Islam 'occupied' a home along with his wife and children. When they ceased to occupy it, he ceased to occupy it also and he was therefore intentionally homeless. Men from overseas, Lord Denning said, should not bring their wives and children to the UK unless they had arranged permanent accommodation for them. The decision was, however, overruled by the House of Lords in uncompromising terms. Lord Wilberforce said that there was no answer to Islam's claim. The law lords were unanimous that, in considering the question of available accommodation, no notice should have been taken of former accommodation overseas.[31]

But the connection between immigration and housing went beyond such questions of whether people were entitled to public housing. In 1979, at the same time as the DHSS had suggested to hospital staff that they had a role to play in the enforcement of the rules on eligibility for free treatment, so the Department of the Environment suggested to local authority departments that they contact the Home Office where an applicant's immigration status was in doubt. In a letter to the Association of Metropolitan Authorities the Department of Environment said:

> There will be occasions on which an authority thinks it appropriate to ask to see documents relating to an applicant's presence, and possibly his passport . . . if . . . an authority finds reason to believe that an immigration offence has been committed or that a breach of the immigration rules may have taken place . . . they would no doubt wish to consider whether they should draw it to the attention of the Immigration Department or the police.[32]

Shortly after this statement was issued, the India Centre for advice and welfare in Woolwich, south London, took up the case of a family which it had referred to the homeless persons section of the local council. The family claimed that the interviewing officer had demanded to see their passports and on inspecting them had told the father that he was an illegal entrant and could be deported. The chairman of the housing committee denied that there had been any accusation of illegality, but defended the request for passports as the 'appropriate requirement . . . to have proof of residence'. In 1980 a Spaniard who had lived in the UK for two years was arrested as an illegal entrant after making an application to Ealing Council's homeless persons section. They had contacted the Home Office to ascertain the man's immigration status and in the process divulged his name and address. The Home Office passed the information to the police who then made the arrest.[33]

In the London Borough of Camden, however, a successful campaign was waged to persuade the local authority not to ask for passports and not to contact the Home Office. Responding to complaints by Camden Committee for Community Relations, the director of housing was categorical on the question of referral to the police or the immigration authorities, saying:

> I certainly do not see it as our duty to alert these authorities to some hypothetical offence that may or may not have been committed by an applicant for housing. Interviewers do not make decisions of this nature, and I would regard any such notification as a gross breach of confidentiality.

Subsequently the council's housing management committee accepted recommendations to the effect that, while the homeless persons section should retain the discretion to ask for a passport when considering a request for housing, this would only be done when the information could not be obtained from any other source. The section would not approach the Home Office for proof of residential status but would ask applicants to provide their own evidence, referring them, where appropriate, to independent advice agencies. The link between the council and the Home Office was thereby broken.

People who are homeless can still be subject to other forms of internal control if they are placed by the local authority in bed and breakfast accommodation. This came to light in 1984 when a London homeless persons section sent a man to a local hotel. He was refused admission because he was unable to supply his passport number. The hotel claimed that the police had instructed them to maintain a register of all guests with particulars of their nationality and passport number. The Metropolitan Police confirmed that such an instruction had been issued and that they made checks on hotel registers. According to the police the instruction had been made under the Immigration (Hotels Records) Order of 1972 made under the Immigration Act of 1971. Until then it had been thought that the Order was used solely to keep track of foreign visitors, but the incident shows that it is also being used as a means of surveillance and internal control.[34]

Housing departments may also demand to see the passports of those who apply for housing other than as homeless people. For example, in Brent, north London, it was reported that in 1979 Asian families were being asked to show their passports before being housed.[35] In Camden during the same year a number of Bengalis who were to be rehoused were told to produce their passports along with their council rent books. It was claimed that this was because of confusion with Muslim names. One of the men objected that he could produce proof of identity with his driving licence and that a passport was unnecessary. He was told that if he did not produce his passport the council would be unable to help him, whereupon he produced it and three or four pages were then photocopied. This was later justified by the director of housing on the ground that this would 'avoid having to ask for proof of identity on any future occasion'. Camden Committee for Community Relations, which had taken up the issue, described this reply as 'unacceptable'. It succeeded in persuading the council to instruct staff not to request passports as a means of identification since this had not been the practice for white tenants and the examination of passports might 'bring back unpleasant memories of immigration procedures which do not exist for the indigenous population'.

Other councils have also been known to ask for passports. In Haringey, north London, for example, the assistant housing officer admitted that the practice had been a 'bit routine here because it seemed so convenient', but the practice was later stopped.[36] An enquiry by the Commission for Racial Equality into the housing of work permit holders found that some local authorities in London had a practice of asking people 'who appeared to be foreigners' to produce their passports, even though all the information which a local authority required could be obtained from a number of other documents. In Newham, east London, passports were also asked for and the practice was only stopped under pressure, again from a local advice agency.[37]

The purpose of such checks has usually been to confirm identity and to establish residential status, since many local authorities will not consider housing anyone who has a time limit on their stay in the UK. Nevertheless, an investigation by the Commission for Racial Equality concluded that the London boroughs of Barnet and Kensington and Chelsea were indirectly discriminating contrary to the Race Relations Act by refusing to offer permanent accommodation to work permit holders until they became permanently resident. Furthermore, the investigation found that the Greater London Council had also been discriminating by refusing to accept work permit holders nominated to their homeless housing quota by the London boroughs.[38]

The use made of passports by housing departments has not however been limited to deciding who may be eligible for council housing. In one case, a black man who applied for housing in the London borough of Southwark was visited soon afterwards by immigration officers and was subsequently deported for having overstayed his permission to live in the UK. In Birmingham, an Asian man was questioned by immigration officers after a visit to the housing department, although his status was found to be in order. In both cases, housing officials had voluntarily informed the Home Office about their suspicions.

The connections between housing and immigration control are therefore extensive. The checking of passports is commonplace for those seeking housing as homeless people, while such checking can also occur when people seek council accommodation in 'normal' circumstances. And as the two cases just cited show, the checking of passports can lead to direct liaison between housing officials and the Home Office. Even where the legality of someone's stay has not been in question, housing officials may still try and evade their responsibility by defining them as outside the scope of the law or regulations.

## Social security

Increasingly during this period, immigration control was extended to the administration of the various forms of welfare benefit. In 1977, for instance, the Labour government announced the end of child tax allowances and their replacement by child benefit. This benefit was to be payable only in respect of children *in* the UK. Those who had children living overseas would receive nothing, even if those children were awaiting entry clearance to come and live in the UK. Under pressure, child tax allowances for children overseas were continued until 1982, but there was no concession made on the payment of child benefit for those overseas and even the tax allowances were considerably reduced in the final year.

The main supplementary benefits legislation made no exclusions of any class of immigrant from receiving benefit, although the secret 'A' code of instructions to staff did stipulate certain classes who would be refused benefit under the extensive discretion afforded to staff. But in 1980 the new Social Security Act and the regulations made under it, excluded from benefit anyone who was in the country without leave or with only limited leave where one of the conditions of that leave was not to have recourse to public funds. The 1980 changes also provided for the refusal of benefit to people who had been sponsored to come to the UK – usually dependants – and to enforce the liability to maintain on to the sponsor where a written undertaking was made. It became a criminal offence for a sponsor persistently to refuse or neglect to maintain someone sponsored.

While the vast majority of people settled in the UK are entitled to claim supplementary benefit and may do so without fear that this may affect their immigration status, the 1980 changes excluded several categories of people from benefit. Such people are therefore expected to manage on the generosity of friends and relatives or, if this is not possible, to leave the country. These categories included not just people who are in the country only temporarily, such as visitors or working holiday makers, but people who will eventually settle permanently in the UK. For example, the immigration rules state that fiancés of British citizens should be admitted to the UK for three months in the first instance, with an extension of 12 months after the marriage. During the period before the marriage they are prohibited from having 'recourse to public funds', including supplementary benefit. Indeed they may not claim supplementary benefit until they have received the Home Office letter varying their leave to 12 months. Similarly, most work permit holders may not claim supplementary benefit since they are not considered to be available for work, yet many will eventually become settled in the UK.

The 1980 changes also excluded from benefit people who are overstayers, subject to a deportation order or illegal entrants. Yet as we have seen, these categories are not as straightforward as may at first appear. This is particularly true of the notion of 'illegal entrant', and cases may be drawn out for years while someone contests the Home Office allegation that she or he is an illegal entrant. The case of Parveen Khan provides a clear illustration of the problem. She arrived in the UK at the age of 19 to marry Shaukat Khan who had arrived in Britain in 1972 when he was 13. Shaukat entered with a relative as the son of another person. In August 1979, four days after Parveen's arrival in the UK, the couple were married and in October Parveen applied to remain here permanently by virtue of her marriage.

At the same time Shaukat consulted solicitors who told him that he was technically an illegal entrant. He was wrongly advised there was a government amnesty in force, which in fact had ended in 1978. The solicitors applied for the amnesty they mistakenly thought still existed, thus alerting the Home Office to Shaukat's illegal status. In 1980, the House of Lords ruling in the *Zamir* case also put Parveen at risk. After a series of interviews, the Khans were told in November 1981 that they were to be removed as illegal entrants, although nothing was said about their two children who had been born in Britain and who could not therefore be deported or removed. Campaigners for the family succeeded in obtaining a postponement of the removal for several weeks, but in February 1982 Shaukat Khan went into hiding and Parveen was told that she was to be removed at the end of the month. Another reprieve was granted but this only marked the start of what Parveen Khan's lawyer described as a 'war of attrition'.

Within a few weeks, Parveen was refused all supplementary benefit and her child benefit was also cut off. In addition, she had to suffer frequent unannounced searches of her home by police officers looking for her husband. The DHSS claimed that Parveen was an illegal entrant and therefore not entitled to supplementary benefit. Even after the House of Lords ruling in the case of *Khawaja* (see page 45) the DHSS continued to refuse benefit; it was only after the Home Office accepted that Parveen was not an illegal entrant, that benefit payments began to be made. The Home Office maintained that it was in 'no way responsible for and exercised no influence in' the DHSS decision to withdraw payments. Despite this unlikely explanation, the Home Office and the DHSS between them had deprived Parveen of any rights. She was unable to appeal against the Home Office decision that she was an illegal entrant, while this ruling was used to deprive her of all welfare benefits. This was in effect an attempt to starve Parveen out of the country. If the Home Office could not actually remove her forcibly, it could, through the DHSS, make life so intolerable that she would be forced to leave. It was only the generosity of supporters, relatives and friends which enabled the Khans to stand up to this pressure.

Parveen Khan was alleged to be an illegal entrant, but the DHSS has behaved in a similar way in cases involving people alleged to be overstayers. For example, 'Jane', a woman dealt with by JCWI, was living in the UK when the Immigration Act came into force. She did not know that her status was irregular and so made no application to have it rectified, although had she done so she would have been granted indefinite leave to remain. After Jane had been here for nine years, her mother became very seriously ill and Jane returned to her country of origin to care for her. While she was there she was told that she would have to obtain entry clearance before she returned to the UK. This was refused and eventually in desperation Jane accepted the offer of a visitor's visa and returned to the UK. Jane had no job and claimed supplementary benefit; this was stopped when her leave expired because the DHSS regarded her as an 'overstayer'. As in the case of Parveen Khan, the Home Office and the DHSS worked closely together, the DHSS acting on the basis of information supplied by the Home Office. Benefit payments were only resumed when the Home Office was persuaded to revoke Jane's conditions of stay.[39]

In another case a Nigerian woman was refused benefit because she had not applied for an extension of her leave while she was recovering in hospital from a difficult pregnancy. She had left her husband, who had persistently assaulted her, and was without any means of support save for donations provided by a local advice agency. She was eventually forced to return to Nigeria, borrowing money to pay her fare.[40]

The 1980 regulations concerning the refusal of benefit to the different categories of people also mean that social security officials have the power to demand claimants' passports. The DHSS internal manual of instructions says that staff should not automatically ask for the passports of people who have 'come from abroad' but should question claimants and 'request passports only if normal questioning fails to remove doubt about a claimaint's status'.[41] One of the problems, of course, is how DHSS staff decide that someone has 'come from abroad'.

The evidence suggests that anyone who is black, for example, or who does not speak fluent English, may well be assumed by DHSS staff to have come from abroad and be asked for a passport. Take, for example, the case of Mohammed Fazan in Sheffield. He came to the UK 25 years ago and worked in a factory until he was made redundant. He claimed benefit and was twice told that he would not receive any payments until he proved his right to be in the country by producing his passport. It was only following pressure and publicity that the DHSS agreed to make a payment, although officials maintained that they had a right to see passports.[42]

More important perhaps than the practice of passport checking by social security offices is the effect which claiming benefit can have on a person's immigration status. The majority of people in the UK can, of course, claim supplementary benefit without any fear that their status may be affected. This includes British citizens, people who have settled status, refugees and people admitted under the special voucher scheme set up for the admission of UK passport holders from East Africa. Even in these cases, however, there may be problems over sponsorship. For example, someone who is claiming supplementary benefit will not be able to sponsor dependants to join them in the UK if one of the requirements of such sponsorship is not to have recourse to public funds. In addition, a sponsor who fails to support a sponsored person can be convicted of a criminal offence and could be deported if they were not a British citizen or a patrial when the British Nationality Act came into force in 1983 (see page 65).

Other people have to consider what effect claiming benefit might have on their immigration status. DHSS staff are instructed to notify their headquarters about claims for supplementary benefit by immigrants. This information is then passed on to the Home Office who can then decide whether a claimant is breaking any condition attached to his or her stay. When the claimant applies for an extension of leave or change of conditions, or makes an immigration appeal, this can then be taken into consideration. Nasreen Akhtar, for example, appealed against a decision to deport her after the break up of her marriage. The adjudicator who heard the appeal not only used the occasion to vent his prejudices about arranged marriages, but also said that he believed Nasreen's claim for supplementary benefit as evidence of her intention to live on social security 'for so long as she can'. Not surprisingly, he dismissed her appeal, although his decision was later overturned by the Immigration Appeal Tribunal.[43]

Social security offices may also in certain cases contact the police or immigration authorities themselves directly. A survey carried out by Janet Garner for Oldham Council for Racial Equality in 1983 found that Lothian Community Relations Council had been told by the DHSS that while personal social security records were regarded as confidential and not normally disclosed to third parties, there were exceptions 'where public interest requires it'. DHSS officers might notice from a claimant's passport that there was some immigration irregularity and 'if there is enough evidence to suggest that the applicant is in the country illegally the information is passed to the Home Office Immigration Service'. The same survey noted that the community relations council in Luton quoted examples where claimants in their area had been visited by the police or the immigration service after they had returned home from an interview at their local DHSS office.

Whether DHSS staff are officially instructed to pass information on to the immigration authorities is not known, but in the context of a climate of suspicion towards black people, such policing of the immigration laws by the DHSS is to be expected. Interpretations of the benefit rules have also become ever more restrictive. One of the worst such cases occurred in 1981 when an Indian woman was refused supplementary benefit because she could not speak English and therefore was not 'available for work'. The decision by the DHSS to refuse benefits was upheld by an appeals tribunal and was only reversed on appeal to a Social Security Commissioner.[44] In another case, the DHSS office in Dewsbury refused benefits to a man admitted as a fiancé, on the ground that he had been sponsored by his father-in-law. Yet the man had married by the date of his claim and was therefore entitled to claim in his own right.[45]

## Conclusion

In many ways, then, immigration and the welfare state have become intertwined. Welfare state officials have become involved in the enforcement of immigration controls in a number of ways. They may be ordered to check on immigration status, as the DHSS staff instruction manual requires. They may be encouraged to check on status and inform the immigration authorities of any suspected irregularity, as the Department of Environment suggests in relation to housing. They may simply respond to a climate of opinion which suggests that it is their duty to act as enforcing agents of immigration control. Such developments have been among the most insidious in the whole issue of internal control for they have masked the real nature of such controls, hiding, as it were, control behind welfare. This has resulted in social security clerks, hospital administrators, college officials and housing officers being turned into immigration officers and informants. But more importantly, it has led to a fear of harassment among many black people, who do not claim benefits or services to which they are entitled for fear that their status and eligibility too, may be called into question. For them, the welfare state has become increasingly an agency of control and harassment.

# 5. Towards the society of surveillance

The nature of immigration control has changed since the passing of the 1971 Immigration Act. In the early 1970s it was still primarily a matter of control on entry – of keeping people out of the country. Untold damage continues to be done through the separation of husbands and wives, the division of families and other consequences of control. But the Act contained the means to develop a fully-fledged system of post-entry controls (although, as we saw in Chapter 1, the seeds of such controls were contained in earlier legislation). Immigration control has increasingly entailed the growth of controls and surveillance of those already here. To this end, the police and the immigration services have been given ever-increasing resources, both in terms of personnel and technology. The role of the police in the enforcement of immigration laws has been extended and, most insidiously, the welfare state and other public services have become increasingly harnessed to immigration control and their officials turned into quasi-immigration officers and informants.

It appears likely that in the next few years there will be further developments in the enforcement of internal control. Already, a decision has been made to introduce a computerised, machine-readable passport as part of the INDECS programme of computerising immigration control (see Chapter 3). This decision has been taken despite a government commitment in 1979 that no decision would be taken on the concept, first mooted by the International Civil Aviation Organisation in 1969, until maximum publicity had been given to the proposal and public comment received.[1] In fact, there has been no such publicity and no invitation for public comment.

Following the 1979 report of a Home Office working party on the subject, the Home Office ordered a number of specimen machine-readable passports from a Derby firm which specialised in the printing of bank cards, security passes and similar products. In March 1981, the government announced that it had decided in principle to adopt a machine-readable passport 'as soon as possible' and that this would be combined with the development of a common-format EEC passport.[2]

Once the machine-readable passport is in operation, immigration officers will be able to find not just the details of the holder but also additional information supplied by the computer once the passport is 'keyed in'. The passport holder will remain ignorant of the contents and accuracy of this information, which will come, in particular, from the computerised immigration 'suspects index'. This index is a list of people 'in respect of whom immigration officers are required to take certain action', according to instructions to immigration staff. It was not intended to be part of the INDECS programme. A decision was made by the Home Office, however, to include it without any reference to parliament and to combine this with the development of the machine-readable passport.

At present the index is compiled manually and comprises about 18,000 names, the maximum which can be handled manually. Computerisation will facilitate the handling of far greater numbers. Indeed, this is anticipated by the immigration service in an internal memorandum seen by the trade magazine, *Computing*. Computerisation will also allow the suspects index to be amalgamated with the 'short list' of suspects supplied to immigration officers by MI5, the security service, and the police. These lists include categories of people on whose movements MI5 wish to be kept informed. They include people in possession of communist or other 'subversive' literature, passengers resident in the UK whose passports contain visas for Cuba or China, and Japanese passengers whose passports indicate travel in the Middle East. In addition to this flow of information from MI5 to the immigration service, the computerisation programme will also provide the means for the flow of information the other way – from the immigration service to MI5, which has its own computer system at its Mayfair headquarters, and to the Police National

Computer and the Metropolitan Police 'C' Department's computer. In short, as *Computing* magazine concluded, 'it provides the framework upon which other surveillance functions can be built'.[3]

The machine-readable passport is to be introduced in Britain in 1987. In 1983 Heathrow Airport installed an experimental terminal for machine-readable passports issued in the United States. By the end of the 1980s most European countries will be using machine-readable passports. All of the computer systems involved in immigration control, except the police systems, have been developed without any external scrutiny and have become public knowledge only through articles by investigative journalists. None, for instance, were in existence at the time of the government-appointed Lindop committee's investigation of data protection. Yet, as we have seen, at least one of these systems – the Immigration Service Intelligence Unit at Harmondsworth – has a capability which the Lindop Committee explicitly drew attention to as presenting 'special problems of definition and control'.

Governments have not been particularly forthcoming on matters connected with this new technology of immigration control. Statements by government ministers that the various parts of the immigration computer system would not be linked have been contradicted by internal Home Office documents seen by journalists. Thus one such paper states that, 'the computer systems might be linked to form a distributed network encompassing the whole country with the centre of the network located at the Home Office ADP Unit in Merseyside'. Only the month before this paper was written, the Home Secretary, in what *Computing* described as an 'incomplete and misleading reply' had told MPs: 'The equipment will be entirely self-contained at Heathrow and will not be connected to any other system.'[4]

The most blatant attempt to shield the immigration computer system from public scrutiny was the proposed exemption from the provisions of the Data Protection Act 1984. The Bill, as published in 1983, intended to make four categories of data exempt: the detection of crime, the apprehension of offenders, the collection of taxes, and the control of immigration. The subjects of records would have had no opportunity to see, and if necessary correct, computerised information if this would prejudice, for example, the control of immigration. The Home Office would have been able to obtain from data banks information about people who were subject to immigration control, without the transfer being registered. This exemption was removed from the Bill only after pressure resulting from press revelations about the immigration computer system. But the exemption for the police remained and included their immigration records. In the same way, the exemption for 'national security' remained and presumably this exempts all records held by the police Special Branch. Since breaches of the immigration law are also criminal offences, these will be covered by the exemption for the prevention of crime. Overall, it seems that the immigration exemption from the data protection law remains in substance, if not in name.

At the same time as it was protecting the police from the limited control of the data protection legislation, the government considerably increased police powers to obtain more information. The Police and Criminal Evidence Act 1984 gives the police wide powers to search premises and seize evidence of a 'serious arrestable offence'. This power will be used to investigate immigration offences and will further increase police information gathering and surveillance. But such increased formal powers will not be the only, or even the most important, way in which the police will increase their surveillance. The routine gathering of low-level intelligence by the police will also expand as greater emphasis is placed on 'pre-emptive' policing. This entails the collection of intelligence about 'targeted' individuals, groups and areas defined by the police as likely to be involved in crime. New information technology will come into its own, resulting in a vast increase in the collection and flow of data, which will facilitate the handling of a volume of information unthinkable in manual systems.

At the same time, the computerised national insurance card is being issued, initially to immigrants seeking work, as well as to school leavers. Such a card introduces new dimensions of unease. The checking of claims for benefits could become much easier, a greater number of officials will have ready access to claimants' records, while the data protection law will offer little safeguard against the leakage of information to third parties.

In short, the technology already exists, at least in embryonic form, for the greater implementation of internal controls to be developed more fully in future. There is nothing to stop the linking of the various computer systems involved or even their linking with the computer systems of the police, MI5 and even the agencies of the welfare state. The machine-readable passport, or the national insurance card, could at some point in the future, provide the key to a whole network of information held about individuals by various agencies and departments and to the greater surveillance of those thought to be subject to immigration control.

The nature of immigration control has therefore changed radically. In the years after the end of the Second World War, black people were actively sought for employment in the UK. As the labour shortage receded and economic growth began to turn into decline, controls tailored immigration more closely to the needs of the labour market. Eventually Commonwealth immigration was stopped altogether, apart from dependants and a few other categories. But the ending of black immigration did not safeguard jobs for people who were in Britain, and as unemployment has risen, so attention has turned increasingly to black people already in Britain. Their labour is no longer needed and they have become a 'surplus population'. The enforcement of immigration controls therefore turns increasingly inwards, to those already here. The new philosophy of control – that it is necessary to preserve the 'British way of life' – points to a solution – repatriation.

Britain is not unique in this respect and there are many parallels with other European countries, especially France and West Germany. Their economies too have relied heavily on labour from other countries. The crucial difference is that European migrants have not been citizens of the country to which they migrated, unlike people from the Commonwealth who were citizens of the UK and Colonies. It was possible for the French and West German governments not only to end new immigration, but also to curtail the stay of many of those previously admitted. Unemployment could be exported, cushioning the French and West German working classes against its effects. But this cushioning could only last for a time and as unemployment increased greater efforts have been made to enforce controls against people in the country and, equally important, to encourage their departure, often by substantial financial inducements.[5]

It has been a common mistake to regard repatriation as something which has to be enforced and therefore as quite impractical and unlikely, the daydream of the fascist right. As the French and German experiences clearly show, repatriation need not be of this kind and can instead be encouraged or 'induced'.

This has been a constant theme of Enoch Powell and, more recently, the far right of the Tory party itself. Consistently, Powell has argued for 're-emigration' brought about, if necessary, by substantial financial incentives. In a speech in Birmingham in 1968 he maintained that ending immigration and encouraging re-emigration hung together 'logically and humanly, as two aspects of the same approach'; and in a speech to the Tory party conference the same year he called for a policy of assisted repatriation and resettlement to be put into effect 'with generosity, with humanity, with determination and with hope'.[6] Ten years later, Powell made it quite clear that repatriation need not be compulsory or enforced.

Questioned by Robin Day on the BBC programme, 'A Question of Immigration', shortly after the publication of the 1978 Select Committee report recommending an inquiry into a system of internal controls, Powell said that 'something like a million' black people would have to be 'accepted back into the countries of which they, including their children born here, are citizens'. When asked whether he advocated compulsory repatriation, Powell replied: 'If by compulsion you mean physical force, no. If in compulsion you include inducement . . .'.[7]

This idea of 'induced repatriation' has been picked up increasingly by the Tory right since then. Several Conservative MPs have pressured the government to extend the existing provisions for repratriation contained in the 1971 Immigration Act. This is often presented as some form of 'aid' to the individuals concerned and the countries to which they are being encouraged to go. Powell, for example, told a packed fringe meeting at the 1982 Tory party conference that the training of unemployed black youths should be geared to the needs of their 'home countries' and Jill Knight has suggested that 'if people have no job here, they are perhaps keen to go back to sit in the sun'.[8]

Although the government announced changes in the repatriation provisions in January 1984, these fell far short of what the Tory right had been advocating. They did not, for instance, make any provision for resettlement grants, although they did relax the conditions under which people might receive state assistance to leave the UK.

Nevertheless, one should not be complacent about the support or sympathy for repatriation which does exist in mainstream conservative circles. The apparently influential *Salisbury Review*, for example, carried in its very first issue an article by Cambridge fellow John Casey, suggesting that the status of black people should be retrospectively altered to that of guest workers 'who would eventually return to their countries of origin with their pension benefits, property and perhaps a large measure of compensation out of public funds'.[9] One-time adviser to Margaret Thatcher and the head of her policy unit at 10 Downing Street, Ferdinand Mount, took Powell to task in 1981, not for advocating repatriation but, apparently, for the way in which he went about it. If, Mount wrote:

> the answers to fears about mass immigration is – and always was – to provide 'voluntary, orderly, humane and even generous' repatriation for those who want it, then the correct order of play was *first* to set up such a scheme, quietly and calmly, and not to start off by inflaming those fears further.[10]

Even though government ministers have emphasised the impracticability of repatriation on a large scale it is quite possible that a government could be pressured into increasing substantially its assistance to people who 'voluntarily' wished to leave the UK. This could happen, for example, in the aftermath of any future serious urban rioting, such as occurred during 1981.

In the current climate, non-financial inducements to repatriation seem more significant. Since the 1960s this climate has developed various components: an ever-increasing level of hostility from politicians and the media, as evinced in discussions about immigration; the stereotyping of black people as 'muggers', scroungers and people who try to get round immigration control;

racial violence and harassment on the streets and the housing estates; structural discrimination and inequality, particularly in employment and housing; and, of course, the operation of immigration laws which divide wives from their husbands and children from their parents. The internal controls described in this book add a whole new dimension to this climate in challenging the rights of black people to welfare benefits and services – or to be in the country at all. Such controls affect not just people who are actually immigrants, but all black people, who are assumed to be immigrants and therefore subject to suspicion.

The alternative (if such it can be called) to induced repatriation is to accept a status which is essentially second class and inferior to that enjoyed by white British citizens. It means accepting that you can be asked for your passport and even arrested by the police, questioned at work, or interrogated about your status at hospitals, schools, colleges and social security offices, simply because you are black.

The implications of this for the wider society are considerable. Firstly, the operation of internal controls and the move towards induced repatriation has fuelled and strengthened popular racism, deepening the divisions between black and white and therefore weakening considerably the possibility of any united political action. Secondly, the operation of internal controls and the kind of treatment meted out to black people, whether by the police, social security offices, hospitals or employers, sets a precedent for such treatment to be given to other groups defined either as criminal, dissident, or marginal.

To put it bluntly, what the police do to Britain's black communities one day, they will do to some other minority the next. It is arguable, for example, that the passport raids carried out by the police and immigration service set a precedent and made it easier for the police to carry out 'Operation Major', the 1982 raid on social security claimants in Oxford during which 283 people were arrested. Many of them, like those arrested in passport raids, were later released without charge.[11]

Over the past few years there has emerged a growing concern about police powers and discretion, arbitrary police behaviour and the lack of any real accountability of the police for their actions. There has been similar concern about the growth of the powers of the executive, the role of the courts in interpreting the law to the detriment of individual liberty, and the increase in surveillance and information gathering by the state. Yet, such issues have been raised for black people, very directly and for many years, through the operation of Britain's internal immigration controls. The serious threats posed in each of these areas might have been more effectively resisted if they had been fought when they first arose in the context of immigration control.

What is to be done about internal immigration controls? In the first place, immigration could be, and ought to be, decriminalised, that is, it should not be part of the criminal law. This was argued in evidence to the Royal Commission on Criminal Procedure in 1979 by the Joint Council for the Welfare of Immigrants. The Council said that, as far as possible, the police should be removed from their role in the enforcement of immigration control and that, except in a few cases (for example, large scale organised evasion of control), the criminal law ought not to be concerned with the control of immigration. Such decriminalisation would also have an important *symbolic* effect in that it would serve to emphasise that breaches of immigration law did not in any sense represent the serious threat to society which crime in the ordinary sense did. Both JCWI and the Institute of Race Relations also pointed out that the role of the police in the enforcement of immigration control had affected police attitudes towards black people generally. The Institute, recommending the repeal of the penal and criminal provisions of the Immigration Act, said that:

> these provisions make every black person in this country a potential suspect in the eyes of the police, and the harassment and suffering they create for many people is not justified by the number of 'real' illegal entrants detained. Also we believe that these provisions help create an attitude towards black people which is incompatible with the police's functions of protecting all sections of the community.[12]

Similarly, JCWI argued that:

> a major cause of the suspicion and mistrust with which the police are viewed by many within the immigrant community,

is the role given to the police in the enforcement of immigration control.[13]

Such decriminalisation would therefore put an end to passport raids and passport checking by the police. People who entered or remained in the UK in breach of immigration laws would be dealt with by administrative measures which would be reviewable in the courts.

Decriminalisation would also put an end to passport raids on workplaces and would also thereby end the need which some employers feel to check the immigration status of their employees. Passport checking at work could therefore be ended, for, as we saw in Chapter 3, there is no legal reason why an employer needs to know the immigration status of an employee.

In the field of education, there should be no question of passport checking either at schools or colleges. Parents wishing to send their children to school could be told as a matter of course that schools are under no obligation to educate people in the country for less than six months but there should be no further investigation of someone's entitlement. In higher education, the situation is more complicated because of the distinction between 'home' and 'overseas' students. The simplest course of action would be to end the distinction and to treat all students alike, thus ending any connection between immigration status and education. If, however, the distinction is maintained, then local education authorities and higher education establishments do need to know who is (and who is not) an 'overseas' student. If this is defined clearly, then questions can be devised which provide local authorities with the information they need to make a decision. But there should be no question of passport checking or investigating someone's immigration status.

In the health service, internal controls could be ended simply by returning to the pre-1982 situation whereby everyone in the UK was entitled to health service treatment without charge, including visitors who became ill while they were here who were entitled to treatment under the so-called 'Good Samaritan' policy. (As we saw in Chapter 4, there is simply no evidence to show that this policy was abused in any significant way.) At the same time, there would have to be the strictest rules, backed by equally strict enforcement, on the confidentiality of information and a complete prohibition on the passing of information about patients to the immigration authorities.

In the area of housing, most current passport checking is simply unnecessary and, quite possibly, unlawfully discriminatory, and local campaigns in some areas have been successful in putting an end to the practice. In some cases, however, particularly those involving housing under the homeless persons provisions, the checking of passports is common and indeed encouraged by central government, as is the passing of information to the immigration authorities. Yet, as the campaign in Camden on this issue showed (see page 86), such checking is not necessary for a local authority to discharge its responsibilities and information required can invariably be documented in other ways. Again, there is a need for strict rules on the confidentiality of information and a strict bar on the passing of information to the immigration authorities. Where it appears to local authority officials that an applicant may be in breach of the law, s/he should be referred to an independent legal advice centre for advice on the regularisation of his/her position.

In the case of social security, the connections between immigration and entitlements are extensive and passport checking may be required as a result. The two areas should be completely separated. Benefits and services should be available to all who declare themselves eligible without any additional checking on black and overseas claimants. People who make a fraudulent claim can in any case be dealt with under the existing law. Such changes will only be possible if many more people begin to understand the nature of internal immigration controls and take the issue on board.

There are now signs that this may be starting to happen, that an increasing, though still small, number of people are becoming aware of the issue of internal controls. There is, however, a danger that challenging internal controls may be reduced to a matter of challenging particular practices and particular policies, ignoring the *politics* from which these emanate. Such practices and policies must, of course, be challenged, but there has to be a simultaneous challenge to the politics of internal control. As we have seen, such politics define black people as the problem and justify the implementation of immigration controls on the ground that immigration control is good for race relations. Now such politics, which continue to define black people as the problem, are increasingly concerned with black people already here. They are in Britain, but not part of it, or as one Tory ideologue Peregrine Worsthorne, has put it:

> Although Britain is a multi-racial society, it is still very far from being a multi-racial nation. Its heart does not beat as one.[14]

Not ony are black people increasingly associated at an everyday level with all manner of problems, for example, crime and education, but they are excluded from the idea of the 'nation' and shown to hold to values, beliefs and customs which are not 'British'. The politics of immigration move increasingly to the solution that blacks must either become 'like us', submitting in Worsthorne's phrase to 'compulsory incorporation' and the acceptance of the dominant values of white society, or, if they do not, they should 'go home'. Such politics have to be addressed, both in ideology and in practice, if internal controls are to be combated effectively.

# Chronology of internal control

1813 East India Company obliged to provide food and accommodation for Asian seamen before they are taken back to India.

1823 Lascars not allowed to be discharged in Britain.

1849 Act passed making lascars British nationals while on board ship.

1894 Articles signed with lascars to require them to return to their countries of origin; ships' masters or owners can be fined if Asian or African seamen found destitute or convicted of vagrancy within six months of discharge in Britain.

1905 Immigration officers given power to refuse entry to those regarded as 'undesirable'. Home Secretary given power to deport following a court recommendation.

1914 Extensive controls on entry and departure of aliens; aliens also required to register with the police.

1919 Aliens prohibited from sitting on juries; criminal offence for aliens to 'incite industrial unrest'.

1920 Home Secretary given power to deport on ground of 'conducive to the public good'. Immigration officers empowered to remove aliens who have avoided immigration control.

1925 Alien seamen required to register with the police.

1962 Power to deport Commonwealth citizens following court recommendation after conviction. Commonwealth citizens can be removed if they have entered after being refused permission, but only if apprehended within 24 hours.

1968 All those subject to immigration control must submit to examination on entry; failure to do so amounts to illegal entry.

1969   Compulsory entry clearance certificates introduced. Home Secretary may deport any immigrant who breaks a condition attached to stay.

1971   Commonwealth citizens arriving after 1973 become liable to deportation no matter how long they live in UK; Home Secretary given power to deport Commonwealth citizens on ground of 'conducive to the public good'; 'family deportation' introduced; power to remove illegal entrants, no matter how long they have lived in UK; police given wide powers of arrest without warrant.

1973   Immigration Act 1971 comes into effect; courts decide it is retrospective. Police Illegal Immigration Intelligence Unit becomes operational; major passport raids.

1974   Passport checks reported in Ealing schools.

1976   Home Office and courts widen definition of illegal entrant; EEC draft directive on workplace controls published. Passport checking in Leicester hospital.

1977   Government 'think tank' recommends enquiry into creation of formal internal controls. Department of Education begins to redefine meaning of 'ordinary residence'. Child benefit scheme announced but not for children abroad.

1978   Parliamentary Select Committee calls for tougher enforcement of immigration law and an inquiry into formal internal controls. Margaret Thatcher makes 'swamping' statement as Tories adopt tougher immigration policy. Industrial tribunal rules that passport checking is not discriminatory. London borough refuses to house black homeless family.

1979   Royal Commission on Criminal Procedure warned of harm done to police/community relations by involvement of police in immigration control. Department of Environment suggests to local authorities that they pass information to immigration authorities. Department of Health and Social Security makes similar suggestion to NHS staff.

1980   House of Lords ruling in *Zamir* takes meaning of illegal entry to its widest point. Removals of alleged illegals reaches highest level. Major passport raids in London and elsewhere. Social Security Act increases connection between immigration control and entitlement to benefit.

1981 Government announces intention to charge 'people from overseas' for use of the NHS. Court of Appeal rules that someone with a house in Bangladesh cannot claim to be homeless. Indian woman refused benefit because she does not speak English and is therefore 'not available for work'. Decisions are later overruled.

1982 Charges for use of the NHS by 'overseas visitors' introduced. Cases of passport checking in housing and social security documented by No Pass Laws Here Group. Pilot scheme to monitor ethnic origin of unemployed takes place amid protests.

1983 Government attempts to exempt immigration control from the new data protection law. Experimental computer system to read passports begins operation.

# References

*Abbreviations:* AC=Appeal Courts, All ER=All England Reports, CA=Court of Appeal, Crim. LR=Criminal Law Reports, HC=House of Commons paper, HL=House of Lords paper, HO=Home Office, Imm. AR=Immigration Appeal Reports, IRR=Institute of Race Relations, PRO=Public Record Office, WLR=Weekly Law Reports.

## Introduction

1. *Financial Times*, 22 March 1978.

## 1. Origins

1. *House of Lords Select Committee on Navigation Laws* (232), 1847.
2. Public Record Office (PRO) file, HO 45/11017.
3. PRO, HO 45/11897.
4. Kenneth Little, *Negroes in Britain*, Kegan Paul, 1947.
5. Andrew Nicol, *Illegal Entrants*, Runnymede Trust/Joint Council for the Welfare of Immigrants, 1981, p. 12.
6. *Ibid.*, p. 13.
7. *Ibid.*, p. 13.
8. PRO, HO 45/11907, quoted in *ibid.*, pp. 42–3.
9. A. Sivanandan, 'Race, class and the state' in *A Different Hunger: Writings on Black Resistance*, Pluto Press, 1982, p. 106.
10. *Ibid.*, p. 106.

## 2. Foundations of control

1. A. Sivanandan, 'Race, class and the state' in *A Different Hunger: Writings on Black Resistance*, Pluto Press, 1982, p. 107.
2. *Ibid.*, p. 107.
3. (1974) AC, p. 18.
4. Ian MacDonald, *Immigration Law and Practice in the United Kingdom*, Butterworth, 1983, p. 396.
5. *Ibid.*, p. 397.
6. Quoted in Andrew Nicol: *Illegal Entrants*, Runnymede Trust/Joint Council for the Welfare of Immigrants, 1981, p. 30.
7. Nicol, *op. cit.*, p. 29.
8. (1976) 1 WLR, p. 97.
9. (1976), Crim. LR, p. 246.
10. (1977) 1 WLR, p. 466, CA.
11. (1978) 1 WLR, p. 700.
12. MacDonald, *op. cit.*, p. 379.
13. *Control of Immigration Statistics 1982*, Cmnd 8944, HMSO, 1983.
14. (1976) 3 All ER, p. 604.
15. (1976) 3 All ER, p. 611.
16. Home Office press release, 4 October 1972, emphasis added.
17. *Daily Express*, 4 July 1970, quoted in *Race Today*, December 1970.
18. *Race Today*, January 1974.
19. *Race Today*, March 1976.
20. Letter to the Joint Council for the Welfare of Immigrants, 4 February 1978.
21. Letter to the Joint Council for the Welfare of Immigrants, 20 January 1978.
22. *Times*, 24 July 1973.
23. *Guardian*, 7 May 1974.
24. *Race Today*, January 1974.
25. *Ibid*.
26. *Hansard*, 19 June 1973.
27. *Times*, 17 January 1972.

28. *Daily Telegraph*, 26 May 1973.
29. *Daily Mirror*, 10 December 1971, quoted in Roger Bohning: *The Migration of Workers in the United Kingdom and the European Community*, Oxford University Press/Institute of Race Relations, 1972, p. 132.
30. *Ibid.*, p. 154.
31. HL, 91, HMSO, 1977.
32. Evidence to the Select Committee on Race Relations and Immigration, HC 410, HMSO, 1978.
33. *Official Journal of the European Communities*, 10 October 1978.
34. *Consultation on Migration Policies vis-a-vis Third Countries*, 1979.
35. Minutes of the TUC Hotel and Catering Industry Committee, 19 April 1978.
36. Letter to Runnymede Trust from TUC, 13 February 1981.
37. See Campaign Against Racism and Fascism (CARF): *Southall: the Birth of a Black Community*, Institute of Race Relations/Southall Rights, 1981, for an account of bussing and other racist education practices in Southall.
38. *Race Today*, January 1974.
39. Quoted in the *Guardian*, 15 March 1980.
40. *Times*, 8 September 1976.

## 3. The system takes shape

1. *Immigration*, HC, p. 303, HMSO, 1978.
2. Robert Moore, *Racism and Black Resistance in Britain*, Pluto Press, 1975.
3. *Ibid.*
4. *Review of Overseas Representation*, HMSO, 1977.
5. *Op. cit.*, para. 160.
6. *Op. cit.*, para. 142.
7. 'From immigration control to induced repatriation', in *A Different Hunger: Writings on Black Resistance*, Pluto Press, 1982, p. 137.
8. (1978) Imm. AR, p. 76.
9. Andrew Nicol: *Illegal Entrants*, Runnymede Trust/Joint Council for the Welfare of Immigrants, 1981, p. 35.

10. *Ibid.*, p.21.
11. Quoted in Ian MacDonald: *Immigration Law and Practice in the United Kingdom*, Butterworth, 1983, p. 419.
12. *Control of Immigration Statistics 1082*, Cmnd 8944, HMSO, 1983.
13. *Times Law Report*, 14 January 1983; for examples of cases see Paul Gordon: *Deportation and Removals*, Runnymede Trust, 1984.
14. *Hansard*, 30 June 1980.
15. Cmnd 7341, HMSO, 1978, para. 8.23.
16. Duncan Campbell: 'Society under Surveillance' in Peter Hain (ed): *Policing the Police*, Vol. 2, John Calder, 1980.
17. *Hansard*, 16 March 1983.
18. *Computing*, 10 February 1983.
19. *Ibid*.
20. Cmnd 7341, HMSO, 1978, para. 3.15.
21. *Computing*, 10 February 1983.
22. *Hansard*, 4 December 1979.
23. *Hansard*, 3 April 1981.
24. See *Computing*, 10 February 1983.
25. *Guardian*, 27 January 1978.
26. Letter to Camden Committee for Community Relations from Brynmor John, Minister of State at the Home Office, 19 October 1978.
27. *CARF*, No. 6, no date.
28. Letter to Camden Committee for Community Relations from Brynmor John, 11 April 1979.
29. *Hansard*, 28 October 1980.
30. Quoted in the *Guardian*, 7 July 1980.
31. *Hansard*, 2 July 1980.
32. Home Office press release, 11 July 1980.
33. *Hansard*, 24 March 1981.
34. *Home Office Circular*, 131/1980.
35. *Times*, 3 April 1981; *Time Out*, 24 April 1981.
36. Letter to Camden Committee for Community Relations from Timothy Raison, Minister of State at the Home Office, 12 June 1981.
37. *JCWI Annual Report*, 1980/81.
38. Letter to JCWI from Brynmor John, 21 April 1979.

39. *Times*, 28 October 1980.
40. *Immigration Law and Practice in the United Kingdom*, Butterworth, 1983, p. 329.
41. *Hansard*, 28 April 1980.
42. *Immigrant Voice*, No. 5, October 1978.
43. Letter to Scottish Council for Civil Liberties from Scottish Office, 23 October 1979.
44. *Police Against Black People*, IRR, 1979.
45. *Guardian*, 8 January 1982.
46. *Waltham Forest Guardian*, 10 December 1982.
47. *Daily Telegraph*, 8 January 1983.
48. Immigration Rules, HC 238, HMSO, 1977, para. 47.
49. Joint Council for the Welfare of Immigrants: *Checks on Immigrant Marriages*, 1977.
50. *Police Review*, 13 July 1979.
51. *JCWI Bulletin*, Vol. 1, No. 6, October/November 1983.
52. *Guardian*, 19 October 1983.
53. HO, 115/1979.
54. *Police Review*, 13 July 1979.
55. Letter, 13 September 1979.
56. Letter from the Home Office to the JCWI, dated 13 September 1979.
57. *JCWI Annual Report*, 1982/3.
58. *Guardian*, 16 August 1980.
59. *Police Against Black People*, IRR, 1979.
60. *Evidence to the Royal Commission on Criminal Procedure*, 1979.
61. 'Skin', London Weekend Television, 23 October 1980.
62. *Ibid.*
63. *CARF*, No. 9, 1979.
64. *No Pass Laws Here Bulletin*, No. 4, October 1982.
65. Letter to Eric Deakins, MP, from Lord Gowrie, Minister of State at the Department of Employment, 25 November 1980.
66. *Control of Immigration Statistics 1982*, Cmnd 8944, HMSO, 1983.

## 4. Second-class claimants

1. *Immigrant Voice*, No. 5, October 1978.
2. *Guardian*, 28 April 1980.
3. *Guardian*, 31 October 1981.
4. *Times Law Report*, 14 May 1981.
5. *Times Law Report*, 6 November 1981.
6. *Times Law Report*, 17 December 1982.
7. For a full account of this issue see Judith Beale and Alan Parker: *Overseas Students: Grants and Fees*, Runnymede Trust, 1984.
8. *Guardian*, 27 February 1980.
9. Letter to JCWI from Home Office, 21 September 1978.
10. *No Pass Laws Here Bulletin*, No. 3, June 1982.
11. 'Gatecrashers', DHSS, 3 October 1979.
12. *Hansard*, 12 December 1979.
13. *Hansard*, 22 January 1980.
14. *New Statesman*, 11 July 1980.
15. *Guardian*, 17 March 1980.
16. *Hansard*, 2 April 1980.
17. *Guardian*, 16 June 1980.
18. *Guardian*, 28 May 1981.
19. *Guardian*, 30 May 1981.
20. *Guardian*, 29 May 1981.
21. *NHS Charges for Overseas Visitors*, HC, 121, HMSO, 1982.
22. *JCWI Annual Report*, 1982/3.
23. *Daily Telegraph*, 9 December 1982.
24. *Daily Telegraph*, 29 April 1983.
25. *Daily Telegraph*, 5 January 1983.
26. *Hansard*, 17 November 1983.
27. *Sunday Times*, 12 November 1978.
28. *Daily Mail*, 28 April 1978.
29. *Times Law Report*, 13 December 1979.
30. *Times Law Report*, 11 July 1980.
31. *Times Law Report*, 20 November 1981.
32. Letter from the Department of Environment to Association of Metropolitan Authorities, 19 October 1979.
33. *Roof*, May/June 1980.
34. Personal communication.

35. *Searchlight*, February 1980.
36. *Guardian*, 18 March 1982.
37. See *No Pass Laws Here Bulletin*, No. 3, June 1982 and No. 6, April 1983 for an account of the campaign in Newham.
38. *The Allocation of Council Housing with Particular Reference to Work Permit Holders: Report of a Formal Investigation*, Commission for Racial Equality, 1982.
39. *JCWI Annual Report*, 1982/3.
40. *Ibid*.
41. *DHSS 'S' Manual*, 1983, para. 3953.
42. *Morning Telegraph*, 4 March 1983.
43. See Paul Gordon: *Deportation and Removals*, Runnymede Trust, 1984, pp. 32–3.
44. *Daily Mail*, 5 July 1982.
45. *No Pass Laws Here Bulletin*, No. 2, March 1982.

## 5. Towards a society of surveillance

1. *Hansard*, 26 July 1979.
2. *Hansard*, 13 March 1981.
3. *Computing*, 10 February 1983.
4. *Ibid*.
5. See Stephen Castles *et al*: *Here for Good: Western Europe's New Ethnic Minorities*, Pluto Press, 1984.
6. Bill Smithies and Peter Fiddick: *Enoch Powell on Immigration*, Sphere, 1969, p. 38.
7. 9 March 1978.
8. *Hansard*, 24 June 1983.
9. *Salisbury Review*, No. 1, Autumn 1982.
10. *Evening Standard*, 10 November 1981.
11. See Ros Franey: *Poor Law*, Campaign for Homeless and Rootless/Child Poverty Action Group/National Council for Civil Liberties/National Association of Probation Officers/Claimants Defence Committee, 1983.
12. *Police Against Black People*, Institute of Race Relations, 1979.
13. *Evidence to the Royal Commission on Criminal Procedure*, Joint Council for the Welfare of Immigrants, 1979,
14. *Sunday Telegraph*, 27 June 1982.

# Index